Sandy Berger's
Great Age Guide to Better Living Through Technology

Contents at a Glance

800 East 96th Street,
Indianapolis, Indiana 46240 USA

Sandy Berger's Great Age Guide to Better Living Through Technology

Copyright © 2006 by Que Publishing

International Standard Book Number: 0-7897-3440-0

Library of Congress Catalog Card Number: 2005922884

Printed in the United States of America

First Printing: September 2005

08   07   06   05   4   3   2   1

Trademarks

Warning and Disclaimer

Bulk Sales

Que Publishing offers excellent discounts on this book when ordered in quantity for bulk purchases or special sales. For more information, please contact

> U.S. Corporate and Government Sales
> 1-800-382-3419
> corpsales@pearsontechgroup.com

For sales outside of the U.S., please contact

> International Sales
> international@pearsoned.com

ASSOCIATE PUBLISHER
Greg Wiegand

ACQUISITIONS EDITOR
Stephanie J. McComb

DEVELOPMENT EDITOR
Laura Norman

MANAGING EDITOR
Charlotte Clapp

PROJECT EDITOR
Daniel Knott

PRODUCTION EDITOR
Heather Wilkins

INDEXER
Chris Barrick

PROOFREADER
Brad Engels

TECHNICAL EDITOR
Teresa Reynolds

PUBLISHING COORDINATOR
Sharry Lee Gregory

BOOK DESIGNER
Anne Jones

Table of Contents

About the Author

Sandy Berger—nationally respected computer authority, journalist, media guest, speaker, and author—has more than three decades of experience as a computer and technology expert.

As president of Computer Living Corp, a computer consulting and training company, Sandy applies her unique ability to explain in easy-to-understand language how to use and enjoy today's technology. Her trademark, Compu-KISS™ (which stands for The Computer World—Keeping It Short and Simple), represents her approach to helping others enhance life through the use of computers and technology.

As primary content provider and host of AARP's Computers and Technology website, Sandy has her finger on the pulse of the boomer and zoomer community. Her feature stories, product reviews, and computer tips have brought a special insight and ease of use to millions of boomers and zoomers.

Sandy writes a monthly column in *Smart Computing* magazine called *TechMates* that reviews two high-tech products that complement each other. She has been a guest on hundreds of radio and television shows, including NBC's *Today Show*, NBC News, CBS News, Fox News, ABC News, WGN, and WOR radio.

Sandy is an excellent example of her own philosophy—use technology, but keep it short and simple. Her previous three books, *How to Have a Meaningful Relationship with Your Computer*, *Your Official Grown-up's Guide to AOL and the Internet*, and *Cyber Savers: Tips and Tricks for Today's Drowning Computer Users*, adhere to these principles.

Sandy is a consumer advocate promoting simplicity, ease-of-use, and stability in consumer technology products. She works with hardware and software developers to help them make their products more user-friendly.

A cum laude graduate of Chicago's DePaul University, Sandy went on to complete intensive IBM training in computer systems, analysis, programming, system operations, and numerous computer languages. She subsequently applied her expertise within several major corporations before founding Computer Living Corp.

Dedication

In memory of Martha Tattersall, my long-time friend and assistant whose life was tragically cut short by a fatal accident. Martha was a boomer who used technology to enhance her life. Her spirit and thoughts live through the writing in this book.

Acknowledgments

As an avid Star Trek fan, I loved the scenes in the Next Generation series where Patrick Stewart who played Captain Picard would say, "Make it so," and the crew would perform whatever tasks were necessary to do just that.

Thanks to Paul Boger, Que's publisher, for putting out the call to "make it so." The "crew" at Que responded in enthusiastic Star Trekien fashion. As you know, producing a book like this takes more than writing. It is a Herculean task for all involved. Thanks to everyone at Que for all their hard work. Thanks to Laura Norman, Charlotte Clapp, Sharry Lee Gregory, Dan Knott, Heather Wilkins, Chris Barrick, and Anne Jones.

Special thanks to Stephanie McComb and Greg Wiegand. Without their vision and dedication, this project would not have come to fruition. Thanks to Judi Taylor and Lisa Jacobson-Brown for all their hard work in promoting the book.

I would also like to thank all the people at Pearson Publishing who supported this project, especially Greg Yurchuck, whose undying support and unadulterated enthusiasm helped to keep me going and whose vision made this series possible.

The people who surround me gave me unlimited help and support. Thanks to the whole gang at Computer Living Corp, to Dana Carroll, and to Teresa Reynolds.

Thanks to my family who is always there for me. My daughter, Marybeth, even though she had a baby while working on this book, continued to help with wording and flow. My other children, Brenda and Michael, were always there to listen and offer support. My husband, Dave, is not only the love of my life, but also my inspiration and my motivation. He is a true visionary and this Great Age series comes from his ideas, thoughts, and dreams. I am happy to be a part of it and to be a part of his life.

We Want to Hear from You!

As the reader of this book, *you* are our most important critic and commentator. We value your opinion and want to know what we're doing right, what we could do better, what areas you'd like to see us publish in, and any other words of wisdom you're willing to pass our way.

As an associate publisher for Que Publishing, I welcome your comments. You can email or write me directly to let me know what you did or didn't like about this book—as well as what we can do to make our books better.

Please note that I cannot help you with technical problems related to the topic of this book. We do have a User Services group, however, where I will forward specific technical questions related to the book.

When you write, please be sure to include this book's title and author as well as your name, email address, and phone number. I will carefully review your comments and share them with the author and editors who worked on the book.

Email: feedback@quepublishing.com

Mail: Greg Wiegand
Associate Publisher
Que Publishing
800 East 96th Street
Indianapolis, IN 46240 USA

For more information about this book or another Que Publishing title, visit our website at www.quepublishing.com. Type the ISBN (excluding hyphens) or the title of a book in the Search field to find the page you're looking for.

Foreword

Written by Jim Stovall
Founder, Narrative Television Network
Award-winning speaker and author

Life is about living each season to its fullest. Each stage becomes the celebration for that which has gone before, and the stepping stones for that which is yet to come. Any age, as Picasso put it, can indeed be a Great Age.

When I was 17 years old, I had a plan for my life which does not even resemble the life I have lived to date. At 17, I wanted to be a high school All American football player, and then I wanted to play on the National Championship college team before moving on to the NFL. I was well on my way to making this a reality when, during a routine physical exam in preparation for college, an eye condition was diagnosed that would result in my eventual blindness. That day, one door closed, and many more opened. I lost my sight, but I gained a vision for who I could and would become.

I remember waking up one morning as a blind person, and the only plan I could think of at that moment involved living the rest of my life in a 9' × 12' room. The thought of traveling millions of miles and speaking to literally millions of people, founding and running a multinational corporation, writing a nationally syndicated newspaper column, or authoring a dozen books—all these things seemed as far off to me then as going to the moon. I sat in my little self-imposed prison and became more depressed and more discouraged as each day went by.

Then technology stepped in, in an amazing way. I am embarrassed to admit that I never read an entire book cover to cover when I had the ability to read with my eyes like you are reading this book now. But as a blind person, since 1988 (thanks to books on tape and a special high-speed tape recorder) I have literally read a book each day. These books have changed my life just like I believe this book from Sandy Berger will change yours.

My life has taken many amazing turns. I have been an Olympic weightlifting champion, become the owner of a Emmy Award–winning television network, and am a successful author and speaker. Now I am pleased to take the next step as my novel, *The Ultimate Gift*, which has sold over two million copies around the world, is being made into a major motion picture. It is a privilege to play a part in delivering messages that change people's lives.

In this Great Age Guide, my friend Sandy Berger delivers knowledge and wisdom that holds the potential—in very practical ways—to change your life now and for years to come. Enjoy!

Have you ever stopped to think about the role of technology in your life? There's no doubt that today's younger generations will benefit from current and future technological advances, but today's older generations are already seeing the biggest lifestyle improvements ever. We are living longer, more active lives than our parents and grandparents. Our ancestors went from youth to middle age to old age. We, with a new mentality and the help of technology, have added an entire epoch to our lives—the Great Age!

Everyone knows that the term baby boomer refers to individuals who were born after World War II. This group is generally recognized as encompassing people who were born between 1946 and 1964. The boomers' older siblings don't have a moniker associated with their generation, but along with the boomers, they are often referred to as zoomers because they are not ready to be relegated to a rocking chair. Boomers and zoomers are zooming into the latter part of their lives, zooming into technology, and zooming into everything they do. They are vibrant individuals who deal enthusiastically with all aspects of their lives. They are ready to enjoy the Great Age they have created.

About Sandy Berger's Great Age Guides

It's about time that someone addressed the issues that face those of us who did not grow up with computers. We are not technologically impaired. We are not dummies. And we are not about to be overlooked.

It's just that we didn't learn about computers in school, so we sometimes approach the new-fangled digital world with a bit of trepidation. Can someone please tell us just what we need to know without the complicated mumbo-jumbo?

That is exactly what this series does. It is explicitly geared for the needs and wants of baby boomers and beyond. It tells you just what you need to know—no more and no less. It uses the winning formula of need-to-know information along with easy-to-understand explanations.

Over the past decade, I have helped many boomers and their older siblings learn how to use computers and technology to enhance and improve their lives. I understand the needs and wants of this generation. After all, I am enjoying the Great Age myself. I am anxious to help guide you into the world of technology where the Great Age is full of enjoyment and anticipation.

Better Living Through Technology

Most of us realize that the path to better living is through technology. Computers and technology now affect every aspect of our lives. They have extended our longevity, improved our health, made travel planning easier, and even made it easier to handle our finances. *Sandy Berger's Great Age Guide to Better Living Through Technology* is filled with information that will enrich your life. It will put you on the cutting edge while making sure that you are far from the bleeding edge. It will help you get comfortable with technology and allow you to understand the many ways that it can make life easier.

This book is intended to give you a taste of the richness and ease that technology can bring to your life. I will give you an idea of what technology can do for you. I hope that this will lead you to explore more possibilities on your own. Websites are given as examples of where you can find more information. Each web address has been checked and rechecked, but if you can't get to a specific website of some reason, just remember that you can probably find many similar websites if you look around.

Remember you don't have to memorize anything here. Just sit back, relax, and absorb whatever information is important to you. This book will give you the gist of what computers and technology can do for you. After you know what is out there for you, you can experience as much or as little as you like. No pressure—just relax and enjoy this book and you will come to enjoy technology.

What's Inside

There are no special instructions for using this book. Start at the beginning or jump around as you please. I've added a quote at the beginning of each chapter because we can always learn from others. I've also included several special features to help you in your quest for knowledge.

Sandy's tip

Sandy's Tips give you my personal tips, tricks, and shortcuts to make life in the digital world a little easier

LINGO

The Lingo boxes explain any high-tech terms in easy-to-understand language.

BLOOPER ALERT

The Blooper Alerts help you avoid some of the pitfalls. By telling you about some of the places where most people stumble, these alerts enable you to stay out of trouble and to feel a whole lot smarter.

Trivia

The Trivia boxes are just for fun. They are tidbits of fascinating information—little things that include today's factoids as well as details from the good old days.

How This Book Is Organized

- Chapter 1, "Becoming a Digital Family," presents ways family members can communicate with each other, create family websites and fun family projects, and even research the family tree.

- Chapter 2, "Search and Learn Online," explains how to use search engines to find what you need. You'll also learn about online encyclopedias, virtual libraries, museums, and other research tools.

- Chapter 3, "Shopping Online for Fun and Savings," brings the digital world of shopping into your living room.

- Chapter 4, "Easy Travel Planning," gives you everything you need to know about travel planning, Internet travel resources, bargains, and discounts.

- Chapter 5, "Managing your Finances," helps you understand online banking, personal finance programs, and investing via the Web.

- Chapter 6, "Digital Photography and Instant Printing," helps you stay up to date in the world of digital cameras, printers, and scanners.

- Chapter 7, "Music, Games, and Digital Diversions" introduces you to the ways that high-tech resources have changed old hobbies, such as music appreciation, cooking, and gardening, and created new ones, such as geocaching.

- Chapter 8, "Online Health Information and Resources," explains high-tech health devices and advances and gives you digital resources for staying healthy.

- Chapter 9, "Meeting People Online," investigates the many ways you can meet people online and have safe and exciting online relationships.

My fondest wish is that you enjoy this book and have fun with technology!

Sandy Berger

Chapter 1

Becoming a Digital Family

The family is one of nature's masterpieces.
—George Santayana

For many families the Internet has become the virtual dinner table. The World Wide Web has revolutionized how relatives communicate and interact with each other. Ten years ago you had to wait two weeks for a letter to get to a family member in Milan. Now an email can be delivered in seconds. With relatives spread across the country or the world, the Internet is the best and cheapest place to keep in touch. Making Web connections between family members is easy with email, Internet telephone, webcams, chat rooms, and instant messaging, and there are plenty of fun activities for family members of all ages on the Web.

IN THIS CHAPTER

- The High-Tech Home
- Communicating with Family Members
- Other Ways to Make the Most of the Internet
- Researching Family History
- Money and Time Saving Tips

The High-Tech Home

As we go through our everyday lives, we might not feel like we live in a high-tech home. After all, most of us are just average folks getting up in the morning, working, pursuing hobbies, traveling, and running errands. Yet all it takes is one good thunderstorm or snowstorm that cuts off the electricity to make us realize how high-tech we really are. Without electricity we don't have heat, lights, or air conditioning. Our televisions, computers, stereos, refrigerators, and microwaves don't work. We can't use our cordless telephones, garage door openers, or security systems.

At a time like this, we suddenly realize technology offers us more than just heat, light, and air conditioning. Technology makes our lives easier and more comfortable. Computers help us get organized. The Internet gives us instant information. We can be in constant communication using cell phones. Digital cameras allow us to snap, edit, and print photos instantly without leaving home. Digital music players give us our choice of music at home or on the go. We have entered an era where technological advances are happening at an accelerated pace. So even though your home is truly high-tech already, in the next 10 years you will see even more mind-boggling breakthroughs.

What Does Digital Really Mean?

The word *digital* is highly used in today's society, but many folks don't really know what digital means. Digital actually describes any system based on *discontinuous* data or events. The important word here is discontinuous, which means not continuous or having breaks. The opposite of digital is analog. *Analog* processes information more or less in a continuous stream. The difference can be easily seen in a clock. An analog clock has hands that circle continuously, simulating a stream of time. Any minute and any fraction of a minute can be represented. For instance, you can look at an analog clock and say with some degree of accuracy that it is one and one half minutes past four o'clock. You can see that the minute hand is half way between one and two minutes. The typical digital clock, which shows the time by flashing the hour and the minute, produces distinct minutes but cannot represent a half of a minute or a quarter of a minute. The digital clock will show that it is one minute past four or two minutes past four. You cannot tell from looking at the clock if it is one and one-half minutes past four or one and one-quarter minutes past four.

From the previous description, you might surmise that analog is more detailed than digital, but that assumption would be incorrect. Although the normal digital clock shows only minutes, a more detailed digital clock can show fractions of minutes—even a thousandth or millionth of a second—something an analog clock cannot do as accurately. Digital equipment can accurately produce even the minutest details. Digital processing is important because a computer or other digital piece of equipment can store and manipulate digital signals quickly and easily.

In addition, analog data can be converted to digital data to create a very high-quality reproduction. This high-quality reproduction is why the entire world is moving toward a digital lifestyle.

To get an idea of the power of digital data, all you have to do is listen to an old analog phonograph record and compare the sound to that of a digital CD. The digital sound quality wins hands down. That's why many of our current devices are digital.

Our computers process information in digital format, as do our digital clocks, digital cameras, and digital music players. And the families who use all of these high-tech devices are certainly digital families.

Communicating with Family Members

When several generations lived together on the family farm, all communication took place face-to-face. Families gathered around the fire in the evening just to relax and talk. Times have changed. Our fast-paced, heavily scheduled lives keep us constantly on the move. Family members are spread around town, across the country, and around the world.

Luckily, computers and the Internet allow us to keep in touch with loved ones.

Happiness is having a large, loving, caring, close-knit family in another city.

—George Burns

Email

Email has become a standard method of family communication. All you need is a computer or email device, such as an MSN TV, and an Internet connection. All the software is already installed on your computer or Internet device. Just connect to the Internet, start your email program, type in the email address of your loved one, and you are ready to send off a quick note. Your email is delivered immediately. Most are delivered within minutes of when they are sent, no matter how much physical distance is between you and your loved one.

LINGO

Instant messaging is a way to communicate in real time with someone across the Internet. A small box on your computer screen tells you which of the friends you have put on your buddy list are online and lets you type private messages to them and receive messages from them.

Instant Messaging

Although email is quick, another type of online communication is even faster. Instant messaging, IM for short, is instantaneous. With IM, you create what is commonly referred to as a Buddy List or Contact List that contains the IM names or email addresses of any family members, friends, or business associates with whom you would like to communicate. The IM software keeps track of these people and notifies you when any of them is online. For instance, you install the IM software, and then put your son on your Buddy List. If you are surfing the Web and your son goes online, a small window pops up to notify you, as shown in Figure 1.1. If you want to send him a message, you simply type it in the box and he will see it immediately on his computer screen. When he responds, it will appear instantaneously on your screen. Most IM software allows you to be detected as online only if you want to be detected. If you prefer not to be disturbed, you can easily block people from seeing that you are online. You can also selectively choose to be seen only by certain individuals.

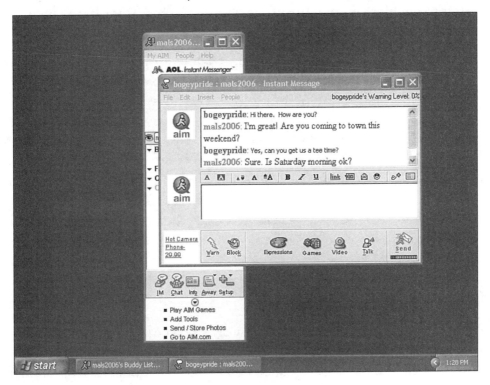

FIGURE 1.1
With AOL Instant Messenger, notes from your friends appear immediately.

Several types of instant messaging software exist, including Windows Messenger, MSN Messenger, AOL Instant Messenger, and Yahoo! Messenger. If you are an America Online (AOL) user, you already have instant messaging software available to you in the form of AOL Instant Messenger. You don't, however, have to be an AOL member to use the AOL Instant Messenger program.

To use this instant exchange of information, the same IM software must be installed on the computers of everyone who is communicating via IM. So, if you use MSN Messenger, Uncle Sal will also need to have that software installed on his computer before you can send him an instant message. Luckily, all of the common IM software is free. Although the most popular IM is text-based like email, video versions are available that enable you to actually see and talk to the other party if a webcam is installed on each end.

There is no cost for the three most popular instant messaging software programs. AOL Instant Messenger (AIM) is available at www.aim.com, MSN Messenger can be found at http://messenger.msn.com, and Yahoo! Messenger can be downloaded at http://messenger.yahoo.com. Mac users can use the instant messaging software that accompanies OS X, called iChat (see Figure 1.2). Because it supports AOL Instant Messenger and Jabber Instant Messenger, you can use it to talk to PC users who have one of these two instant message software programs. iChat can handle text messaging, and with additional equipment like microphone and camera, it can also handle audio and video instant messaging.

Webcams and Video Phones

Want to see your daughter in Europe more often without all those expensive plane tickets? The answer might be a webcam or a video phone. Webcams are small cameras that come in all shapes and sizes. The most popular type sits right on top of or next to your computer. With a webcam you can send live video while chatting online with your instant messaging buddies. Some webcams come with software that even enables you to add video to email messages. Many companies, like Logitech, also have video calling plans so you can use their webcam to call others over the Internet and actually see them as you talk. There is a monthly fee for this service, but it is often less than you would pay for telephone calls between the two parties.

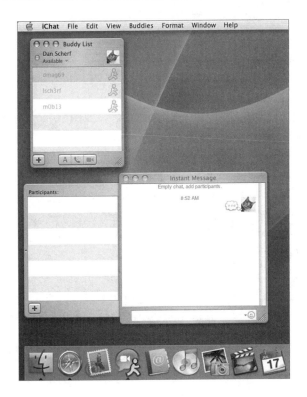

FIGURE 1.2
iChat is instant messaging software for the Mac.

Instant messaging enables you to communicate with your family and all of your friends as well. Microsoft's research shows that the average person knows 290 people. So Microsoft allows you to have 300 people on your MSN Messenger list of buddies.

LINGO

A **webcam** is a camera that allows viewing of live images over the Internet.

There are also video phones that work in a similar manner. Some video phones actually place the call over the Internet. Some use your regular telephone line to make the call. Each person will generally need a video phone of the same type to communicate between two or more parties. Although these devices are expensive right now, prices are falling and the technology is constantly improving.

Sandy's tip
Webcams are posted on street corners, in homes, and in public places around the world. You can see baby lions at the zoo, view the skiers in the French Alps, or watch people as they cross the street in New York City. For listings of webcams, go to WebCam Central (www.camcentral.com) or EarthCam (www.earthcam.com).

Sandy's tip
Some photo websites also allow you to post video clips so you can see that toddler take her first steps and experience the thrill of that first homerun.

Cell Phones

Given the current popularity of cell phones, it is not surprising that families are using them more to communicate. There is no longer any reason to set a meeting point and time when at the mall or the museum. Even if you are visiting these places with the entire family, you can go your separate ways and make contact on the cell phone when you are ready to meet. These types of family communications have become so popular that cellular companies are now offering special discounts to family members and special accounts that allow free calling between family members. If your husband is going by the grocery store on his way home but he has already left the office, you can call and tell him to stop for that loaf of bread. Cell phones do make life easier.

Family Websites and Photo Sites

Becoming a digital family in today's world means using Internet resources to make family life easier and more fun. Whether you just want to share information with your immediate family or you want to bring members of your extended family closer together, there are many web resources to help you.

If you have a computer wiz kid in the family, put her to work creating a family website. If not, don't worry. You can join an online community that will allow you to create a web area where you can post messages, pictures, addresses, and more. These web communities not only provide the website, but also the tools that allow you to easily add to and change your website.

If you want a full-blown family website where you can share photos, post family news, create a family calendar, hold live chats, store family addresses, and share recipes, look at a site such as Your Family Hub at www.yourfamilyhub.com and MyFamily.com at www.myfamily.com. Both give you similar functionality for family coordination and sharing. The Your Family Hub website is shown in Figure 1.3. These websites all charge a fee for their service, but most are pretty inexpensive. Because the cost varies greatly, be sure to check out the fee structure carefully.

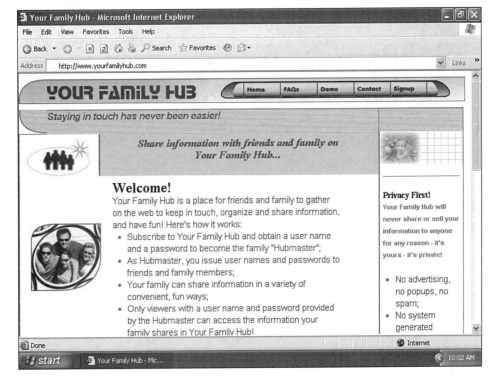

FIGURE 1.3
Create a place to share family photos, news, and events with a family website such as Your Family Hub.

Most of these websites have one family member as the main contact. She grants access to others for the website. Each invited family member gets a username and password. Each one is then allowed to add photos, news, and calendar items. Some sites have different levels of access with different privileges. Before you sign up for a photo-sharing or family website service, be sure to check out its privacy policy.

If you don't need a full-fledged family website but you would like to share your digital photos with other family members, you can join a photo-sharing website. These websites allow you to post family photos to share with other family members. The website provides the tools necessary to post the photos. Usually this is very easy. Then you get an Internet address showing where the photos are located. Email this address to other family members and they simply click on the link to view the photos. Most photo websites also offer photo-editing tools, photo printing services, and personalized paraphernalia such as photo mugs and photo calendars. Some of the most popular photo websites are

Sandy's tip
For a small fee, many photo-sharing websites will turn your digital photos into an impressive customized photo book.

- Kodak EasyShare Gallery at www. kodakgallery.com

- Snapfish at www.snapfish.com

- Club Photo at www.clubphoto.com

- ImageEvent at www.imageevent.com (see Figure 1.4)

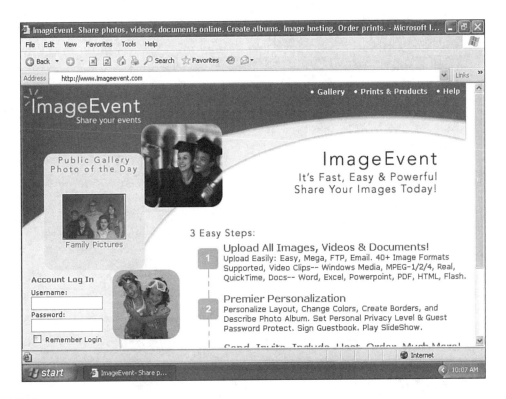

FIGURE 1.4
Share and print family pictures at photo websites such as ImageEvent.

Other Ways to Make the Most of the Internet

The Internet is a great tool for bringing generations together. What is it that grandma and grandpa, the children, and the grandchildren all love to do? They all love to have fun. And the Internet can help.

Hobbies

Hobbies are a great place to begin. Fortunately, there are websites dedicated to just about any hobby you can think of. From scrapbooking to collecting sports memorabilia, the Internet covers them all. It provides research and knowledge for your hobby, and it will also connect you with others who share your interests.

If you don't yet have a dedicated diversion, visit some of the great websites about hobbies and choose a new one that will be interesting to both you and your family. The About website's Hobbies & Games area (http://about.com/hobbies) and eHow (www.ehow.com) are two websites that will whet your appetite (see Figure 1.5). Whether it's model railroading, butterfly collecting, knitting, or cooking, the Internet will prove a valuable resource.

FIGURE 1.5
Get hobby and game ideas at About.com.

Creating Memories with the Youngsters

Promised to baby-sit the grandkids or other younger relatives but you're stuck with a rainy day? The Internet can't make the rain go away, but it can offer some great distractions for the children when they are forced to stay inside. Here are a few sites worth exploring.

Remember the Crayola crayons you played with when you were a kid? Well, Crayola has gone digital with the Crayola website (www. crayola.com). To access this site, you have to register and get a username. The process is free, fast, and worthwhile. After you are in the site, you can choose to print out pictures to color, connect-the-dot pictures, and explore an endless list of craft projects, such as making hats, cards, or boats. You can choose activities by theme—be it Fourth of July or Easter—or by project. You can even send email cards.

Because the Mickey Mouse Club, Howdy Doody, and Romper Room were a part of our younger lives, we can certainly understand how important television characters can be. So if you are looking for something for the kids, try PBS Kids (www.pbskids.com). This is a wonderful site where the children can visit with their favorite TV personalities. Younger children can practice counting with Big Bird from Sesame Street. Slightly older kids can find activities from the show ZOOM. Most of the TV shows offer games, stories, crafts, and music. Don't worry about not recognizing the popular children's TV stars. The kids will let you know by looking at the list if they are more interested in Mister Rogers or Barney! While you are surfing with the youngsters, visit a few other TV channel websites, such as Nick.com (www. nick.com), NickJr.com (www.nickjr.com), and Noggin (www.noggin.com). These are all children's cable television stations that have an excellent web presence. You might even be amazed at how neat some of the latest child icons, such as SpongeBob SquarePants and Dora the Explorer, really are.

Disney Online (www.disney.com) is another must-see for children of all ages. As usual, Disney provides a lot of entertainment options with fantastic animation activities for kids. I would recommend you visit this site before sharing it with the younger ones because it is very busy and inundated with ads for Disney products. Yet after you find some interesting areas, the site will certainly keep the kids busy. Disney also has some wonderful creative software worth investing in if you have kids who love Disney characters.

The bottom line is that if it is popular with kids, it probably has a website. So the next time your niece is upset because she forgot her Barbie doll at home, go to the computer. Do a search or just take a guess at the site name. You'll learn pretty fast that www.barbie.com offers enough activities to make her forget all about her doll.

LINGO

Genealogy is the investigation and study of ancestry and family history. Many people believe that researching your ancestors gives you a better idea of who you are.

Researching Family History

Genealogy, the tracing of a family history, continues to intrigue all generations. Precomputer days, finding an ancestor was a daunting endeavor that could easily take years of work. Genealogists, whether amateur or professional, gathered information from family members and records found at national archives, libraries, and governmental offices. Now the computer is playing an integral role in genealogical research. The computer offers improved means of research, as well as advanced methods of organizing the results of genealogical exploration. Technology has provided the tools to enable genealogists to easily share their research information. This is a huge step in the research process, promoting shared genealogical information on a global scale.

Armed with a computer, an Internet connection, and a good genealogy program, you can now research your family history without leaving home. Technology has made the search for one's roots easier and, in many ways, more gratifying. Several different genealogy software programs are available that have made discovering one's past very easy. Data can be entered using wizards that are built into the program. Although it used to be tedious to document all the people and items in a family tree, these new programs make it easy. After you enter the information, you can view it in many different formats. A child can have multiple sets of parents, an individual can have multiple spouses, you can use estimated dates, and you can change field labels. Many programs offer the ability to create an interactive family tree with photos, sound, and video. All have a large variety of printed reports. Some of the most popular genealogy programs are Family Tree Maker (www.familytreemaker.com), RootsMagic (www.rootsmagic.com), and Legacy Family Tree (www.legacyfamilytree.com).

Many online resources exist to help you find your family. Ancentry.com (www.ancestry.com) has the largest collection of family history resources in the world. At the American Family Immigration History Center (www.ellisisland.org) you can get passenger arrival records. Genealogy.org (www.genealogy.org) has census records, state records, and a listing of other genealogy websites. These resources will also unite you with a huge community of genealogy enthusiasts and experts from around the world. You can get advice from community message boards, professional articles, and chat rooms.

BLOOPER ALERT

When gathering information on your family tree, be sure to make a backup copy of your data.

If you have ever had an attraction to genealogy, there's never been a better time to become involved with this wonderful hobby. Although the Internet has quickly developed into a powerful research tool for genealogists seeking their roots, other benefits have been created for families. Many interesting websites now combine the search for family history with the connectivity of the Internet to offer ways to share all types of family information.

An exciting website for anyone interested in family history is FamilySearch (www.familysearch.org), the website of The Church of Jesus Christ of Latter-day Saints, also called the Mormon Church. Because Mormons consider genealogy a religious mission, they maintain one of the largest collections of genealogy data in the world. This website can, of course, help you find your roots. The interesting thing, however, is that this website will also help you share your family history with others (see Figure 1.6). At this site you can permanently preserve your family history and distribute it to others around the world. Visit the

FamilySearch's Share My Genealogy area to add your genealogy files to the Granite Mountain Records vault, located near Salt Lake City, where they will be archived and made available to others on CD-ROM or through the Internet.

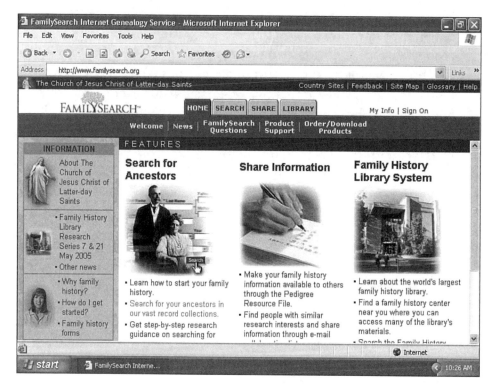

FIGURE 1.6
Search for ancestors and share information at the FamilySearch website.

The popularity of genealogy and the emphasis on family has given rise to a new variety of websites—the community-database combo. *Community-database combo* sites most often link to other genealogy sites and maintain active online bulletin boards for sharing information. When visiting these sites, be prepared to see some advertising. Most sites make money through combinations of membership fees, banner ads, and sales of genealogy software and books.

These sites aim to expand the usual genealogy research activity by offering ways for users to enrich their current family relationships.

Family Tree Maker (www.familytreemaker.com) is one of these sites. It uses its community section to empower everyday people who are interested in genealogy to uncover and share their unique family stories. This site encourages people to create a home page and search through other people's home pages to see if they are researching the same surnames.

Sandy's tip
While most genealogy websites' base level databases are free, access to more detailed, in-depth information often requires registration and sometimes a fee.

At Yourfamily.com (www.yourfamily.com) you can create a family web page, as well as search other family home pages. YourFamily.com invites you to add your family tree to their extensive database. Their bulletin boards might help fill in your family tree and locate long-lost rela-

Trivia
The FamilySearch website, at www.familysearch.org, contains more than 665 million names.

tives. After you have created your own family home page, you can post a taped oral history and heirloom photo albums.

SurnameWeb (www.surnameweb.com) sponsors an online community along with a free website and a free Web-based email account. It gives you tools to announce your website to your friends, inviting them to visit. Other free tools help you improve your search engine ranking and create a press release to deliver to local newspapers. Your guest book is ready for visitors' comments, names, and email addresses.

One site, MyFamily.com (www.myfamily.com), stands out for its full development of the family community concept. Although they offer free online family history software that enables multiple family members to work as a team in updating their family tree, MyFamily.com has taken the family concept well beyond genealogy. MyFamily.com is a password-protected community on the Internet where users can post family news, create family photo albums, hold chats, search for ancestors (see Figure 1.7), and maintain a calendar of family events. The Shops@MyFamily.com area offers private wish lists, email reminders, and personalized gift-giving recommendations. MyFamily.com offers free newsletters on other important family topics, such as cooking, photography, money, health, travel, and more.

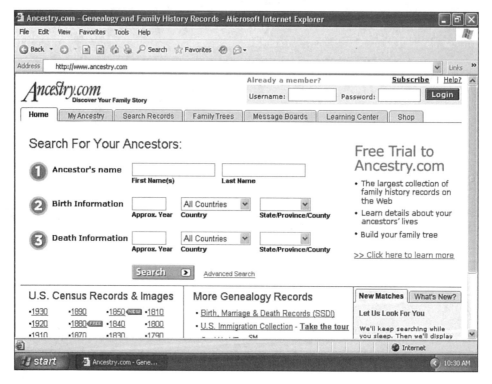

FIGURE 1.7
You can easily trace ancestors using Ancestry.com, which is a part of the MyFamily.com website.

MyFamily.com is just one of a number of community-type websites for families and other groups. Often you will find sites dedicated to various groups, such as high school reunion committees, church organizations, or former military units.

With all these tools just waiting for you, it might be a great time to give in to your genealogical curiosity. Or perhaps you would like to use one of these sites to bring your family closer together.

Money and Time Saving Tips

There's no doubt about it, technology can save us both time and money. It provides speedy communications as well as speedy delivery. Ten years ago if you wanted to get a document to someone outside of your immediate vicinity, it might have taken days. Today you can email or fax the document for immediate delivery.

Technology is saving us money in many unseen ways. New appliances are much more energy efficient than they were a few years ago, resulting in lower energy bills. Fiber optic cabling has lowered telephone costs. Cars get better mileage. A set-back thermostat can automatically adjust the temperature to save you money in heating and cooling costs.

Although a computer and monthly Internet service is a significant investment, your computer and the Internet can actually save you money. Email is much cheaper than long distance telephone calls. Sending pictures by email is less expensive than paying for postage, and it's faster. A computer can save you even more in unexpected ways. For instance, a new set of encyclopedias can easily cost more than $1,000. Yet the same information can be purchased on CD or DVD for use in your computer for less than $100. You might even be able to find much of the same information on the Internet free. Using a digital camera and a computer to inventory your household possessions can pay off royally if you have an insurance claim.

LINGO

The word *Internet* is often shortened to Net and it has spawned several other new words. For instance, a *netizen* is a citizen of the Internet and *netiquette* is etiquette for the Internet.

Here are just a few more ways you can use your computer and the Internet to save money:

✓ Sell your old "treasures" on eBay (www.ebay.com) or any auction website.

✓ Use auction sites to make purchases, as well.

✓ Shop online discount sites, such as Half.com (www.half.com) and Overstock.com (www.overstock.com).

✓ Use comparison shopping sites, such as PriceGrabber.com (www.pricegrabber.com) and Shopzilla (www.shopzilla.com), before you make your purchase.

✓ Compare and purchase airline tickets online. Check out each individual airlines or use sites such as Travelocity (www.travelocity.com), Priceline (www.priceline.com), or Orbitz (www.orbitz.com).

✓ Book hotels and car rentals online. Many websites, such as Priceline, Travelocity, and Orbitz, that compare airline tickets also book hotels and car rentals.

✓ Compare gasoline prices before you fill up your tank. Use sites, such as GasBuddy (www.gasbuddy.com) and GasPriceWatch (www.gaspricewatch.com), to get the gas prices for your local area.

✓ Compare insurance rates online. Check out individual companies as well as comparison sites. Two of the most popular insurance comparison sites are NetQuote at www.netquote.com and Progressive Auto Insurance at www.progressive.com.

✓ Online investing is often cheaper than trading offline. Look at the well-known brokerage houses such as Charles Schwab (www.schwabat.com) and Merrill Lynch (www.ml.com), as well as smaller companies such as Scotttrade (www.scotttrade.com) and E*Trade (www.etrade.com).

✓ Compare rates for home loans. Again, there are comparison websites available, such as LendingTree.com, where you can look at prices from several companies at once.

✓ Check out the cost of that new car before you head to the dealership at Kelley Blue Book (www.kbb.com) or Edmunds.com (www.edmunds.com).

✓ Purchase pet medications, contact lenses, and other items that you might find cheaper online. For instance, Drugstore.com has contact lenses at reduced prices. 1-800-PetMeds at www.1800petmeds.com helps you save money on pet supplies and medications.

✓ Use online resources for simple home repair tips so you don't have to hire a plumber or handyman. You can get tips at HomeDoctor.net (http://homedoctor.net) and Ask the Builder (www.askthebuilder.com)

✓ Design and print your own greeting cards. You'll get a unique handcrafted card at a fraction of the price of a store-bought card. You can purchase greeting card software, such as Hallmark Card Studio by Sierra or PrintMaster by Broderbund. For free card templates, check out some of the printer manufacturer websites such as Epson at www.epson.com and Canon at www.canon.com.

✓ Go online for energy conservation tips. The U.S. Department of Energy has some great tips at www.eere.energy.gov/consumerinfo/ energy_savers.

We all know that time is money. Besides, with so many important things in life, if you can save a little time on mundane chores, your life gets better. Here are a few ways to save time using your computer and Internet connection:

✓ Use online banking and you won't have to make a trip to the bank.

✓ Check out homes online before you head out with the real estate agent.

✓ Take online classes. Most colleges and universities now offer classes you can take without leaving home.

✓ Get weather information (www.weather.com) and sports scores (www.espn.com) online instead of waiting for them to scroll by on the television screen.

✓ Download tax and other governmental forms without leaving home (www.firstgov.gov).

Sandy's tip
If you like to use your local library, the Internet can still be a great resource. Most libraries have online systems you can use to search for and reserve books.

✓ Research everything online and you might never have to go to the library again.

✓ Use online resources to trace your family tree and you'll eliminate trips to dig up birth certificates and old records. Good places to start are www.ancestry.com and www.genealogy.com.

✓ Grocery shop online. Netgrocer (www.netgrocer.com) and Peapod (www.peapod.com) are online grocery stores (see Figure 1.8). Your local grocery store might also have an order-online option that includes delivery to your door.

✓ Use your computer to look up a postal code. The United States Postal Service website at www.usps.com has a free ZIP code lookup.

✓ You can also use your computer and the Internet to perform routing tasks such as stopping and starting mail and newspaper service.

✓ Use a website such as 411.com at www.411.com to find phone numbers or addresses.

✓ Plan your trip ahead of time with a mapping website such as Mapquest (www.mapquest.com) so you won't spend time looking for your destination.

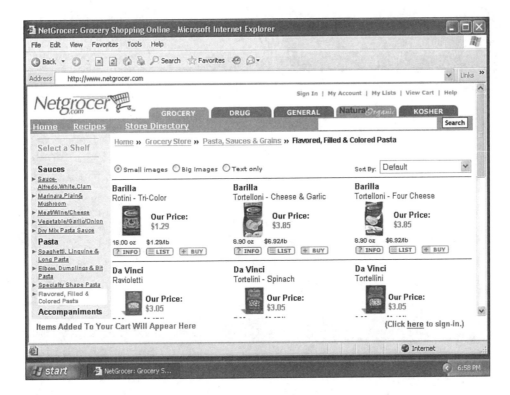

FIGURE 1.8
You can choose your groceries without leaving home with Netgrocer.com.

> ✓ Shop online for that occasional gift and save yourself a trip to the store.

> ✓ Check out online stores for special Web-only offers and free shipping promotions. These can often save you more than coming across a sale at your local mall.

> ✓ Pay your bills online. No need to write a check, put it in an envelope, take it to the post office, and allow three days for it to get there.

Sandy's Summary

Isn't it amazing? When you think about it, you suddenly realize that you are already living in a high-tech home! Today's homes are filled with high-tech wonders such as digital clocks, microwave ovens, televisions, digital blood pressure monitors, and computers. Even our garages hold fully computerized automobiles.

Technology is infiltrating our lives in a good way. It is making life easier. This is especially true when talking about the family. Communicating with family members is easier than ever. We can now use cell phones, email, and instant messaging to bring our families closer together.

Family and photo websites enable you to share family information online easily. Online resources for children can be fun for children of all ages. Computers and the Internet help to bring the generations together by allowing family members to share websites, photos, hobbies, and information. Whether your family is spread around the city or across the world, the Internet can make you feel closer together.

The Internet is also a resource to help you trace your family history and find your roots. Not only is this a great hobby for everyone in the family, but whether Great Uncle Alex was crown prince or a crook, it allows family members to feel closer by understanding where they came from.

Internet resources save you time so you can spend more time with family and friends. Thankfully, they can also help save you money.

I'm happy to see all of you accepting and using technology in your lives. I know it is not always easy, but it is truly a worthwhile endeavor.

Sandy Berger

Chapter 2

Search and Learn Online

Knowledge comes, but wisdom lingers.

—Lord Alfred Tennyson

W hen we were youngsters in school, we studied and learned because being a student was the focal point of our lives. As we grew up and became a little wiser in the ways of the world, we realized that learning is not just for kids. It is a lifelong experience. In life, we learn as we go. Many of us would gladly give up our forty-, fifty-, or sixty-year-old bodies if we had a chance to exchange them for the body we had when we were twenty. Most of us, however, would not be willing to go back to the minds we had at that age. We simply would not want to lose the knowledge and wisdom we have amassed.

It is our grown-up quest to discover new things that help to sharpen our minds, develop our self image, and improve our lives. The best part of learning as an adult is that it is much more fun than "having" to study. We can investigate anything we like, develop special interests, and pursue new avenues of knowledge. Every day of our lives we learn new things, and computers and the Internet have made that pursuit of knowledge more fun and ultimately more interesting than ever before.

The Internet is like having a whole new world of wisdom at your fingertips. Online resources make it easy to access information about anything. Whether you want to pursue a college degree or just find a picture of Tyrannosaurus rex for your grandson, you can now do it easily right from the comfort of your own home. So jump right in and soak up some knowledge as you let the exciting world of online information encompass you.

Understanding and Using Internet Search Engines

There are millions and millions of pages on the Internet. So how do you go about finding information on the subject you are interested in? Luckily there is a marvelous tool that will help you find just about anything. It is commonly referred to as a search engine.

Search engines are simply software tools programmed to search for the information you specify and present that data in a useable format. Some search engines or search tools, like the one built into the Windows operating system (click on Start, then choose Search), can reside on your own computer. However, the search engines that are used to scour the Internet for information are located on the Internet.

LINGO

A **search engine** is an online program that works in a web browser and searches for any information you request. Basically, you tell the search engine what you are looking for by typing in some descriptive words and the search mechanism searches the Web and finds it for you.

LINGO

Query: The word or string of words you type into a search engine. When you tell the search engine what you want to know, you are querying the Web.

Using a Search Engine

A search engine's website typically has a text box where you can enter the terms you are looking for. After you type in the word or words by which you want to search, you press the Enter key on your keyboard or click the button beside the text box (often labeled Search, or sometimes Go). This sends your query to the search engine, which searches its database for occurrences of the text you entered. In a matter of seconds, the search engine returns its results. The results generally appear as a page that lists links to websites containing the words in your query (see Figure 2.1). Search engines do not take you directly to a particular website. Instead, they give a choice of web pages that meet your search criteria and that might be appropriate places for you to find the information for which you are looking.

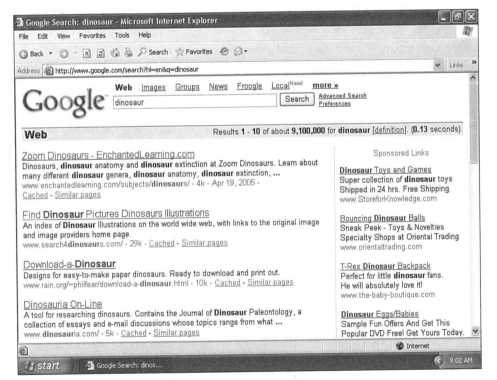

FIGURE 2.1

In Google, the underlined text represents links you can click that will take you to web pages pertaining to your query. Each link gives you a brief description of what the web page is about.

LINGO

A **search utility** or search tool is the page you see when you visit a search website.

Each search engine looks and works a little differently. Some have a list of categories to click on which help you refine your search. Some return their information in different forms. No matter how they work, they usually produce useful results. Search engines are very smart. Many are even able to tell you when you misspell a word in your query. As long as the spelling is not too far off, they are intuitive enough to figure out what you are trying to search for and will return suggested alternative spellings for your search words. For example, if you search for "Taranosaurus Rex," many search engines will politely suggest that you might have meant to search for "Tyrannosaurus Rex" (see Figure 2.2).

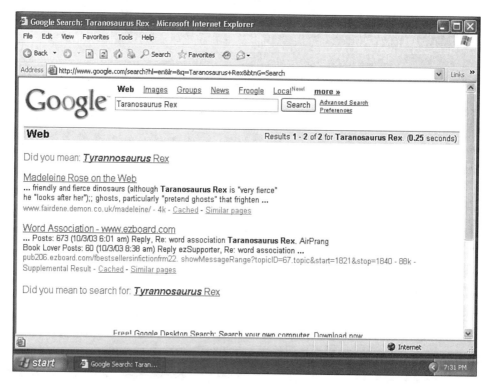

FIGURE 2.2

If you misspell a word, Google often politely suggests the correct spelling.

Finding a Search Engine

Even if you have never used a search engine, it is quite likely that you know the names of several of the most popular ones. You hear their names in the media or from your friends or relatives. Just think for a minute. Haven't you heard of some of these: Google, Yahoo!, MSN, Ask Jeeves, Lycos, and InfoSpace?

These search engines are some of the most popular ones used on the Internet today. If you'd like to visit their websites, simply type the following URLs into your web browser's address bar and press the Enter key on your keyboard:

- Google   www.google.com
- Yahoo!   http://search.yahoo.com
- MSN Search   http://search.msn.com
- Ask Jeeves   www.ask.com
- Lycos   www.lycos.com
- InfoSpace   www.infospace.com

Google

Use Google to search for information about any topic. In the text box, type the word or words related to what you are looking for and Google does a very good job of showing you the websites where you can look for the information you want to find.

Google also allows you to search for other types of information, as shown in Figure 2.3. For example, you can search

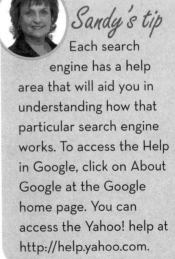

Sandy's tip

Each search engine has a help area that will aid you in understanding how that particular search engine works. To access the Help in Google, click on About Google at the Google home page. You can access the Yahoo! help at http://help.yahoo.com.

for images to go in your next newsletter by clicking the Images link. You can search for groups of people talking about specific subjects, such as how to buy a digital camera or whether to buy or lease their next car, by clicking the Groups link. Google also allows you to search for news sites related to the information you give it. For example, if you click the News link and type in the words *computer viruses*, you will get a list of links for recent news articles about computer viruses.

If you want to go shopping, click the Froogle link and type in the name of an item you would like to purchase, such as a camera phone. In just seconds, you will get a list of links for websites where you can learn about and purchase camera phones. You can use the Local link to find out where that item can be purchased locally. This feature even provides you with an interactive map with driving directions to the specific retailer.

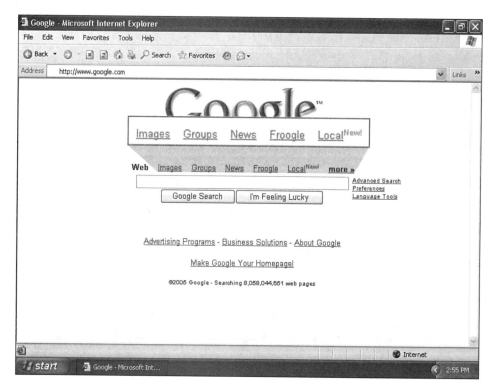

FIGURE 2.3
Google allows you to search for images, groups, news, and other specialized information.

Google is constantly adding new features. Most of these features are tested in an area called the Google Labs that you can find at http://labs.google.com. This is an interesting area. It gives you a preview of new features before they are implemented and also gives you a brief look into the many services that search engines like Google are planning to introduce in the future.

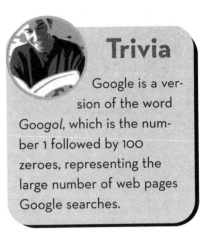

Trivia

Google is a version of the word *Googol*, which is the number 1 followed by 100 zeroes, representing the large number of web pages Google searches.

Yahoo!

Yahoo!'s home page looks quite different from Google's, but it has some of the same features. Using Yahoo!'s text box, you can search for general information and you can also search for images and news. The Local menu choice will take you to a search area specifically made to search businesses in your area. The Products link aids you when you are ready to do a little shopping. Yahoo! search also has a Video link. Type in the name of a current box office movie and press the Enter key. The next page shows you pictures from the movie. Click any picture and you will see a video preview of the movie.

In addition to the text box and the specific searches, Yahoo! also has a directory. You can access the Yahoo! directory at http://dir.yahoo.com or you can find it by clicking on the Browse the Yahoo! Directory link on the Yahoo! home page. The Yahoo! Directory provides a way to search the Web by categories. If you happen to be interested in art, business, entertainment, health, recreation, or science, you can use the directory to find subcategories and to ultimately drill down to specific information. This is a useful type of search when you are looking for general information rather than searching for a specific word or phrase.

MSN Search

MSN's home page has the obligatory text box that most search engines use. Along side the text box is a drop-down menu enabling you to do

Sandy's tip
Although there is technically a difference between a search engine (the actual search mechanism) and a search utility or search tool (the graphical interface you see at a search website), both are commonly referred to as search engines.

more than a general Web search. You can search for news, images, or shopping. You can also search for movies, which is similar to Yahoo!'s video search. If you type the name of a company or a stock symbol, you can search for stock quotes. If you click on Encyclopedia, you can quickly find things in Microsoft's online version of Encarta, a multimedia encyclopedia.

Lycos

Just like the other search engines, Lycos allows you to search for key words and terms. It has separate tabs for News, People, Discussions, and Products. Using the Yellow Pages, you can also search for people, if you need an address or phone number, or for information about businesses, such as addresses, phone numbers, maps, and even driving directions. The Multimedia link helps you search for pictures, audio, or video.

Ask Jeeves

The neatest thing about Ask Jeeves is that Jeeves understands questions (see Figure 2.4). Based on the idea of a British butler, Jeeves is always there to help you. Instead of feeling like you are interacting with your computer, you get the feeling you are being helped by a real person. You can ask Jeeves about anything and he will oblige you by giving you a list of links, not from just one search engine, but from several. Ask Jeeves is a metasearch engine, so Jeeves sends your query to several other search engines at one time. Your results are dramatically improved by the help of Jeeves because you get a combination of links gathered from more than one source. Jeeves also lets you search for pictures, news, products, and local information.

Ask Jeeves has a special service called Ask Jeeves for Kids that includes links to study tools and news resources especially chosen for children. It also has an interesting area called Top Searches where you can see what other people are searching for.

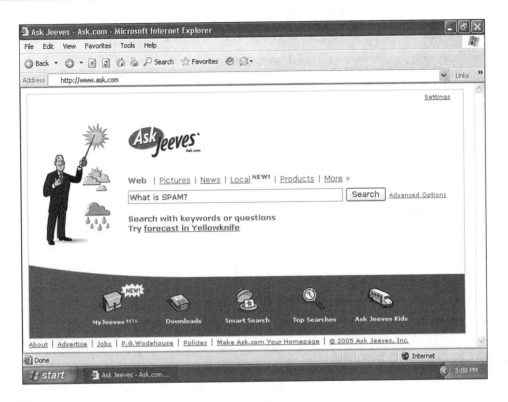

FIGURE 2.4
Ask Jeeves is a website where you can ask a question in plain English.

InfoSpace

InfoSpace is unique in that it searches for people and businesses in the United States through its White and Yellow Page directories. You type in as much information as you know and it does a very good job of finding who or what you are looking for. For instance, go to the White Pages and type in the name of your college roommate and the state in which you think he lives. Even if you aren't sure of the city or the state, InfoSpace will find all the people in its directory with that name, along with their addresses, telephone numbers, and a map of where they live. You can even request driving directions and find out who their neighbors are. InfoSpace also has a feature called Reverse Lookup. If all you have is a phone number or an address, InfoSpace will provide you with the name of the person or business.

Which Search Engine Is for You?

Google, MSN, and Ask Jeeves are all popular search tools and all are very good. If you are just beginning to use search engines, it is best to choose one and learn it well. Every search engine uses different rules and techniques, so pick one search engine and stick with it. Look at the advanced options it offers, check out the help area, and try wording searches differently to compare and evaluate the results.

After you have become accustomed to searching, you can branch out and try other search engines. You might find that Google is best for general searches, InfoSpace is perfect for finding people, and Yahoo! is good for searching by category. Or you might want to use each search engine in succession. For instance, if you are looking for a picture of an elephant and the Google image search comes up short, you can then try the image search in Yahoo! or MSN.

Smart Searching

Because of the enormous number of documents on the Internet, you should learn how to enter the proper words to target the results to your expectations. The following instructions are for Google, one of the most popular and easy-to-use search engines. If you are using a different search engine, check the advanced options or help file to find out exactly how it works.

Choosing Search Words

Carefully consider your search words (also known as search criteria). Be as specific as possible and select the most descriptive words you can think of. Remember, there are many different ways to express the same thing. For instance, if you are looking for garbage, you might also try the words *trash* and *refuse* as well.

Use search words that indicate exactly what you are looking for. For example, you want to learn more about the movie *Jaws*. If you go to a search engine and enter the word *jaws*, you will get some information about the movie, but you also might get information on Jaws, a screen-reading program for the blind, and JAWS, a Women's Journalism group. You can narrow your search results by entering one additional word. Enter the words *jaws movie*. In most search engines, this will give you only websites that have both the word *jaws* and the word *movie*. Google ignores common words such as *of*, *for*, *a*, and *the*. So, you could also enter *jaws the movie* with the same results. Don't worry about capitalization; Google does not differentiate between upper- and lower-case letters.

Double Quotation Marks

Use double quotation marks for phrases and names. This instructs the search engine to treat multiple words as a single term. It will return only web pages where the words inside the quotes are used together in the order given.

Narrow the Search

Narrow your search by using additional terms. When you enter search terms, Google looks for any web page that has all of the words you enter. To limit the search, just add more pertinent words. A search for *George Washington* came up with 17 million results. A search for *George Washington Carver* showed 431,000 links. When I added quotes and searched for *"George Washington Carver,"* it narrowed the results to 176,000. That still sounds like a lot of pages, doesn't it? The trick is to narrow it down even further by entering more words that indicate exactly what you are searching for. If what you really want to know is where George Washington Carver grew up, a search for "George Washington Carver," along with the words *childhood* and *home* would give you any page pertaining to George Washington Carver that also mentions either childhood or home. So entering the search words *"George Washington Carver" childhood home* will give you just what you need.

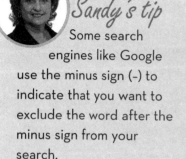

Sandy's tip

Some search engines like Google use the minus sign (-) to indicate that you want to exclude the word after the minus sign from your search.

Minus Sign

Use the minus sign to exclude certain words. When you want all relevant result pages except those containing a certain word, prefix your query word with a minus sign. Google will then ignore all pages containing that word. For instance, enter *Washington -George* to get information about people, places, and things named Washington, but not George. Enter *George -Washington* to get information about others named George, but not Washington. Be sure to put a space before the minus sign but no space after it. The correct entry is George -Washington, not George-Washington.

Advanced Options

Google has an easy-to-fill-in form for advanced searches. Just click on Advanced Search from the Google home page and you can fill in a form that spells out the basis of the results. You can choose to look at only recently updated web pages, web pages written only in your choice of languages, only pages that have the search words in the title, or pages where the search words are found only in the URL. You can even filter your results to delete explicit sexual content. Many of these options have shortcuts, but the advanced options page is great if you are new to searching.

This is just the start. To become an expert Googler, go to the Google website and look at the options. Read its instructions and try a few searches. Before you know it, you will be able to find that needle in the Internet haystack.

Encyclopedias and Dictionaries

The World Wide Web has literally opened up the entire world to us when it comes to learning about any subject. Every imaginable resource on any conceivable topic is at the tip of our fingers. Through the Web we now can access information for which we traditionally have turned to books. There are online dictionaries and encyclopedias, as well as online libraries and museums. You can even complete an entire college degree without ever leaving your computer. Classes are held in virtual classrooms where course materials and lectures are delivered to you through your computer and students and instructors interact entirely through the Internet.

Let's discuss some of the ways in which you can tap into the vast amount of learning materials available on the Web. Books are such a large part of our history and culture that they will never be completely replaced; yet, there are two types of books you don't ever need to buy again: a set of encyclopedias and a dictionary.

Encyclopedias

You might remember browsing through that set of leather-bound encyclopedias, amazed by all of the information they contained. But let's face it. Finding the information you needed in those volumes was not always easy. Often you had to look through book after book to find what you were searching for. Then there were those additional year books which came every year with more current information. Sometimes you had to search through several year books to complete your investigation.

You will also remember how expensive a set of encyclopedias was. Many families spent hundreds of dollars in order to have access to information. Today all the information from those old bound volumes is available in digital format and frees up a lot of space on your bookshelf. Much information from encyclopedias can be accessed on the Internet free. Some encyclopedia websites also offer a wider range of information on a subscription fee basis. Several encyclopedias can be purchased on CD or DVD, allowing you to actually own the encyclopedia in digital format. Even when there is a cost involved, it is often much less than you might have previously paid for a set of encyclopedias. Also consider that these digital reference tools include multimedia features. So you can hear John F. Kennedy's inaugural speech, you can see the lights of Paris from the Eiffel Tower, and you can listen to the National Anthem of Canada—all from the comfort of your chair and in less time than it takes to dig out that old set of encyclopedias.

Encyclopedia Britannica

The Encyclopedia Britannica (www.britannica.com) is known as the Cadillac of encyclopedias. It is an almost boundless research tool. Online encyclopedia access is limited, but you can take advantage of a seven-day free trial offer and unlimited access is easily available for a monthly or yearly subscription fee. Even without subscribing, a wealth of information is available through magazines, newspapers, dictionaries, thesauruses, and other related resource materials at the Britannica website.

Want to see how worthwhile owning a computer can be? Just look at these prices. While the Encyclopedia Britannica Print Set retails for more than $1,000, you can purchase the Britannica Ultimate Reference Suite on CD or DVD for just $69.95. On those computer disks you will find more than 100,000 articles, including all the articles in the Britannica Print Set. You can purchase an entire computer plus the Encyclopedia Britannica software for less than you would pay for the set of printed books.

Microsoft Encarta

Encarta at http://encarta.msn.com was one of the first encyclopedias to contain multimedia features including audio, video, animations, and dynamic maps.

An abridged version of the software containing approximately 4,500 articles is available online. Encarta articles and other media are updated weekly, providing current information on world politics, economics, science, culture, and sports. You can experience Encarta in another language, such as French or Italian, by clicking on Encarta Worldwide. The pages are written in the language of the country you select. Encarta also offers an online virtual globe that can be rotated and magnified. The atlas is interactive, meaning it can be clicked to get more information about a certain region.

You can purchase several versions of the Encarta encyclopedia, which will come on several CDs or DVD. You can also subscribe to the complete online version.

Trivia

The Grolier Encyclopedia was the first encyclopedia to produce an online version. It was also the first to be introduced on CD.

Wikipedia

The Internet has created a free flow of information unlike anything we have ever seen before. The Wikipedia is a great example of this. The word *Wikipedia* is formed from the Hawaiian word *wiki*, meaning quick, and the word *encyclopedia*. Wikipedia is an unusual source of information. It is a free online encyclopedia (http://en.wikipedia.org) that can be edited or added to by anyone. It thus might contain inaccuracies or poorly researched information, but because the content is actively written and debated, it provides a very thought-provoking experience. In addition to encyclopedia entries, Wikipedia also includes information from almanacs, gazetteers, magazines, and current events.

Dictionaries

Do you remember studying vocabulary words every Friday for your weekly English test? Our grammar school teachers did their best to impress upon us the importance of the English language. Of course, they were right. Words are powerful. Using them correctly and understanding their meaning helps us to better understand and relate to others. With online resources, you no longer have to find the dictionary and search through the pages to find the meaning of a word. Instead, you can click over to a dictionary website, type in a word, and get the meaning instantly. An online thesaurus will give you alternative words. You can even continue your learning by visiting some of the dictionary websites that have a Word of the Day feature.

Merriam-Webster

You might recognize the name Merriam-Webster as a name that has been in the reference business since the 1800s. The Merriam-Webster website, at www.m-w.com, is a great place to visit for free information. It has a free online dictionary and thesaurus. The website includes audio pronunciations, Word of the Day, word games, and other English language resources.

> *Sandy's tip*
>
> Both Dictionary.com and Merriam-Webster Online have downloadable tool-bars that allow you to look up words while you surf without having to leave the page you are viewing.

Dictionary.com

Dictionary.com is a free online English dictionary, thesaurus, and reference guide. The crossword puzzles and other word games will keep your word skills sharp. An online translator and help for grammar and usage is also available. For the vocabulary junkie, there is a Word of the Day feature that will email a new word to you every day, along with its meaning and use.

Other Reference Websites

In addition to the traditional dictionaries, dictionary-type websites also provide interesting and useful information other than word definitions. The Biographical Dictionary (www.s9.com/biography) has information including dates and accomplishments for more than 28,000 notable men and women.

Websites such as FreeTranslation.com (www.freetranslation.com) offer free translations for the more common languages, such as French, Spanish, Norwegian, Russian, and Portuguese. You type in text and get a free translation between languages. If you are looking for translation involving other languages, visit Word2Word (www.word2word.com), which currently has almost 200 languages listed with links to dictionaries and translators for those languages.

If you are a word lover, you will want to visit the Online Etymology Dictionary at www.etymonline.com. This free website provides an easy-to-search dictionary of word origins, including single words and phrases. Rather than definitions, etymologies are explanations of where our words came from and how they sounded hundreds of years ago. Did you know that the term "bring home the bacon" was first recorded in 1908? That M.A.S.H. stands for Mobile Army Surgical Hospital? That in 1941 the American term "radar" was chosen instead of the British term "radiolocation" for the newly introduced method of detecting distant objects and determining their position? The Online Etymology Dictionary is chock filled with these and other interesting word facts.

One other interesting resource is the World Factbook. Found at www.cia.gov/cia/publications/factbook, this is a website for world facts related to geography, government, economy, transportation, military, transnational issues, transportation, and communications. It covers all the countries of the world.

Online reference materials include compendiums of quotations, maps, atlases, and online thesauruses. As you surf the Web, you are sure to find other resources as well.

Virtual Museums and Libraries

Hundreds of museums and libraries located all over the world can now be accessed from the Web. Every major museum and library has a web presence. Have you ever wanted to visit the Louvre Museum in Paris? You don't have to book a plane ticket. You can take a virtual tour of the Louvre without ever leaving home. Just surf over to www.louvre.fr. Choose the language you would like to view the website in and then click on Virtual Tour. Explore the architectural views; visit the art, painting, or sculpture galleries; or view the antiquity galleries. Delve into the Louvre's website (see Figure 2.5) and you can find information about its rich history as well as its many collections. There is even an online museum shop where you can purchase prints, sculpture, CDs, DVDs, art books, and jewelry.

Okay, you will not actually be in Paris, but this is one way you can view much of the Louvre without getting blisters on your feet.

FIGURE 2.5
You can visit the Louvre without ever leaving home.

The number of museums in the world is truly amazing. Just visit the Museums Around the World website (http://icom.museum/vlmp/world.html) to see what I mean. This website lists links to hundreds of museums around the world. Whether you are looking for museums to visit on an upcoming trip or you just want to get a feel for the many museums in existence, this website will fit the bill. It has links to all types of museums. The Art Institute in Chicago, the History Museum in Colonial Williamsburg, and the Museo del Prado in Madrid are just a few of the many museums listed at this site.

Libraries

If you spent hours at local libraries when you were growing up, you will want to investigate the many library resources available online. The Library of Congress, shown in Figure 2.6, is the largest library in the world, with more than 500 miles of bookshelves. To get a sample of all that reading material, you can visit the Library of Congress online at www.loc.gov. Many of the Library of Congress's services are available over the Internet, including the Library's online catalog, information about its reading rooms and collections, and tips on how to successfully search its site.

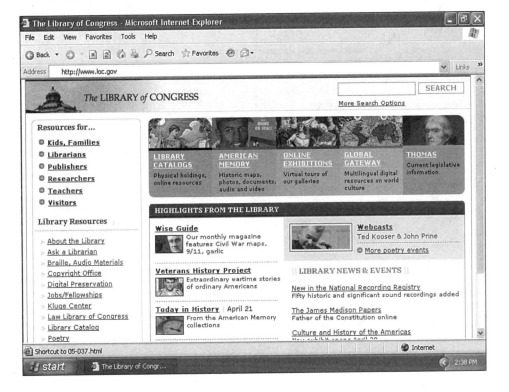

FIGURE 2.6
The Library of Congress website is a treasure trove of information.

If you are interested in history or genealogy, this website will be a treasure. An outstanding collection of U.S. and foreign genealogical and local historical publications are available in the Local History and Genealogy Reading Room (www.loc.gov/rr/genealogy). For the avid genealogist, there is even a list of links to other helpful genealogical sites. There is also a wonderful section with war-related stories from Veterans at www.loc.gov/vets/stories.

The Thomas area of the Library of Congress at http://thomas.loc.gov, named for Thomas Jefferson, is filled with legislative information. At the Thomas site, you can search for information on bills and resolutions, check out current public laws, or read legislative committee reports.

Other areas of the Library of Congress website include online gallery exhibitions, information on U.S. history and culture, and resources on world culture and other digital libraries. For the lifelong learner, this is a not-to-be-missed resource.

When thinking and learning and researching, don't overlook local resources. Although you can still hoof it over to your local library, you might not have to. Public Libraries.com at www.publiclibraries.com has listings for all the public libraries in the United States with web access. Click on any state for information on its public libraries. This site also gives you web access to U.S. state libraries, university and college libraries, presidential libraries, national libraries of the world, medical libraries, and libraries of national archives and records. Each library website varies in its scope and online resources, and some require a library card number for access, but most are worth the visit.

News and Magazines

Remember when your dad put a nickel or dime in your hand and sent you over to the local store to pick up a newspaper? It seems that only the price has changed. The newspaper format, delivery method, and content has pretty much remained static over the last fifty years. All of that is changing as we move into the digital world. I fully expect that before too many years go by our newspapers will appear automatically on our kitchen table each morning. They will be printed with electronic ink on special reusable paper. The news will be beamed to your digital newspaper over a wireless Internet connection. In the mean time, we can get all the news we want online, often without even paying that extra nickel or dime.

Web-Connected Newspapers

Have you ever thought about reading your favorites newspapers online? Thousands of newspapers worldwide have realized that the Internet is a force to be dealt with. Faced with "if you can't lick 'em, join 'em," they have jumped on the Netwagon. Around the world, most major newspapers have developed an Internet presence. To see the extent to which newspapers have joined the online world, you can visit the NewsLink (http://newslink.org). There you will find links to newspapers in the United States, as well as nearly every country in the world. More than 4,000 U.S. newspapers are now online. Another website offering access to online news is www.onlinenewspapers.com. They also list thousands of online newspapers. You might be surprised by the sheer number of newspapers that are available, free of charge, over the Internet.

Best Online Newspapers

Newspapers are finding that online reporting is not necessarily the same as on-the-street reporting. The pressure for online stories is even more intense than ink-and-paper articles. Digital newspapers are constantly faced with updating content and reporting news as it happens. They are also expected to develop deeper, richer content against real-time reporting demands.

Recent surveys have surprisingly revealed that pictures are more important in print newspapers and that people read more of the text when they are reading online. Design of online publications is also very important. Several newspapers that have successfully made the transition over the past few years are *The Washington Post*, *The New York Times*, and *USA Today*, all three of which won an EPpy Award in 2004. The EPpy Awards, presented by *Editor & Publisher* magazine, honor online publications in such categories as "Best Internet News Service" (with more than 1 million monthly visitors: *The Washington Post,* www.wash-ingtonpost.com), "Best Overall Newspaper" (Internet affiliated, with more than 1 million monthly visitors: *The New York Times,* www.nyt.com), and "Best Use of Rich Media" (in an Internet Service with more than 1 million monthly visitors: *USA Today,* www.usatoday.com).

Magazines

The Internet has welcomed the magazine world with open arms. Almost every print publication has an online version or entry point of some kind. Yet each magazine seems to offer differing amounts of information, in different formats. The method taken by a publication for posting its contents online varies from magazine to magazine. Some have only a subscription page online, where you can subscribe to the magazine but cannot read its contents. Others post the entire content of the print magazine on the Web free. Some magazines share special selections from the printed edition online.

One of the latest trends is to offer access to the online magazine information only if you subscribe to the print edition of the magazine. Magazines that do this often have much added value available online, which is a real boon for Internet-connected computer owners.

Because no standard approach has developed, online publications continue to feel their way, trying to find out what business plan works for them. Consumers can rejoice and enjoy the evolution of online magazine publishing, mainly because many magazines are on the Internet free, cover-to-cover. Readers of all ages can benefit. All they have to do is a little research to find out what free information is available.

In an effort to reduce that endless flow of printed magazines to your mailbox and shorten the stack of magazines piled on your coffee table, why not check out your favorite magazines to see if there is an online version. Try typing in the name of the magazine in a search engine. There is a good chance you will find it easily. By using your computer and the online edition of your favorite magazine, you can keep up with the world's happenings, the fashion world, or a special interest. You might even find you can save some money on magazine subscriptions.

News with Online Connections

New ideas for connecting the print world and the online world abound. A few years ago, several magazines, such as *Forbes*, and newspapers, such as *The Post and Courier* in Charleston, S.C., tried a new way to link magazines and newspapers with the online world. The newspapers and magazines in the trial put tiny bar codes in its articles. Readers used a pen-like wand scanner attached to a computer to read the bar code. The computer would then pull up information related to that article from the Web. Although this experiment didn't work as well as expected, you can be sure other ways to tie the offline and online worlds will succeed in the future.

Like newspapers, most television news networks have online versions. For example, Fox News, CNN, ABC, and all the others have active websites that give free news and information. Several Web-based news agencies have also popped up. One of these is Ananova, shown in Figure 2.7.

Ananova is a virtual newscaster created by the British Press Association. At her own website, this somewhat glamorous, wide-eyed 5' 8" digital lady delivers news and breaking news bulletins with a Mid-Atlantic accent. Ananova's green hair, robotic voice, and slightly jerky movements give evidence that she is a computer-generated character; but she is a good one. Programmers have successfully given her three dimensions and a personality. Ananova is programmed to show the expected emotions and actions related to the news articles she is reading. Her expressions and superficial-looking smile are tagged to various words in the articles to help the computer animation program know when she should smile or look serious. To check out Ananova, go to www.ananova.com and click the Video Reports link.

GREAT AGE

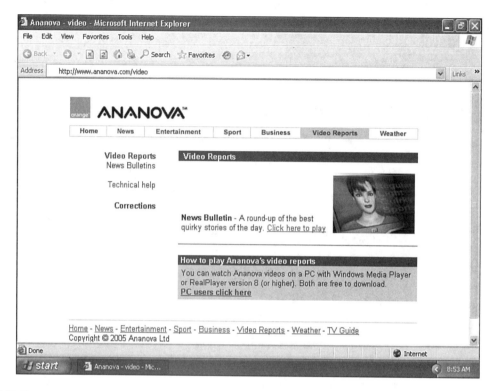

FIGURE 2.7
Ananova is a virtual anchor woman found only in cyberspace.

As more and more people move to high-speed broadband Internet connections, online consumer news and information services are being redesigned for this type of high-bandwidth, highly interactive, continuous access. The emphasis will be on full-motion video, lots of animation, and audio in a more television-like entertainment quality.

Customizing Your News

If you want instant access to certain news sites, several websites allow you to customize an area of their web space so that it delivers the news you want. For example, you can go to Yahoo! and personalize an area of its website called My Yahoo! so that its contents pertain to your interests. You can choose the news, sport scores, stocks, and weather. If you like, you can even add your horoscope. You can then add that page to the list of favorites in your web browser or use it as your Internet browser home page. MSN has a similar personalization page that it calls MyMSN. Some of these websites even let you choose the colors that will appear when you view your customized web page.

Blogs

A blog is a personal journal that is posted on the Web. The word blog comes from Web Log. Blogging has become a very popular pastime, with many bloggers adding to their blogs on a daily basis. Blogs usually focus on a certain subject. There are political blogs, blogs about hobbies, and blogs that focus on many other subjects.

Blogs are like chatter in cyberspace. Although they are often real journalistic offerings, they have a certain immediacy that makes them more like talk radio than newspapers or magazines.

LINGO

A *blog* is a personal journal that is posted on the Web. The word *blog* comes from web log.

There are thousands of blogs on the Internet. You can find them by using a search engine. You can also use a blog aggregator like Bloglines (www.bloglines. com). Bloglines is a free service that allows you to search and subscribe to blogs, news, and online content. Bloglines boasts that "it is the most comprehensive, integrated [online] service for searching, subscribing, publishing, and sharing news."

There is no software to download or install. Simply register as a new user and you can instantly begin accessing your account, at any time, from any computer or mobile device. Bloglines is a window to a whole new world of dynamic content that is being created and distributed over the new "live" web. You can personalize your own news pages, and tailor them to your interests.

Bloglines helps you subscribe to and manage a lot of news and information. You tell Bloglines what you are interested in and it tracks the information, retrieves new information as it happens, and even organizes it for you on your own personal web news page. Each news source is called a *feed*. You simply search for the content you are interested in and identify the feeds you want to track. After you subscribe to those feeds, which in most cases requires a single click, Bloglines will constantly check those feeds for changes or additions and direct new information onto your Bloglines personal page.

The most popular website of its kind, Bloglines indexes more than 300 million blog entries a day. It offers unmatched features for consumers of online news and information and the people and organizations that publish syndicated web content.

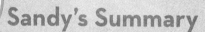

Sandy's Summary

They say using the proper tool for the job gets the work done faster and easier. Nowhere is this more true than when you are looking for information on the Internet. With the Internet, however, you not only have to use the right tool—a search engine—but you have to know how to use it properly.

Anyone can use a search engine with varying degrees of success. If, however, you take the time to learn and understand how search engines work and what they do, you will be rewarded with the ability to find just what you need, exactly when you need it. After you know that there are several types of search engines and that you can use different search engines to find different things, you are on your way to "smart searching."

With the copious amount of information on the Internet, learning how to search for information will be rewarding, and using the Internet to quench your life-long thirst for learning will be invigorating.

Sandy Berger

Chapter 3

Shopping Online for Fun and Savings

When prosperity comes, do not use all of it.

—Confucius

Forget crowded malls, endless parking lots, and long lines. From groceries to gifts, you can buy just about anything online. Online shopping can save you time and money. You can use special websites called comparison shopping sites to find the best price for any given item. Although Internet shopping won't completely replace window shopping at the mall, when you know exactly what you want, online shopping can't be beat. It is also perfect for when you need to send something across the miles. Need a shower present for your niece in Chicago? Order online. Have the company gift wrap the present and insert a gift card with your own personalized message. No trip to the mall. No trek to the post office. What could be easier?

IN THIS CHAPTER

- Safe and Secure Shopping
- Using Shopping Carts
- Online Catalogs and Auctions

Trivia

The largest shopping mall in the United States, the Mall of America in Minnesota, has more than 2.5 million square feet of retail space, but the Internet carries more products.

Safe and Secure Shopping

Nervous about shopping online? You are not alone. Many people enter the world of online purchases with trepidation. Yet, as each year passes, more and more people overcome their anxieties and jump online to make purchases. Nothing is completely safe, but online shopping has proven itself with millions of transactions being safely processed each day.

There are a few simple things you need to do to make sure that your online shopping is safe and secure. The first is in choosing trustworthy companies. Because credit card fraud takes a bite out of their bottom lines, most reputable companies have devoted a great deal of effort to ensure your shopping experience is enjoyable, your personal information is safeguarded, and your transactions are secure.

Finding a Reputable Company

LINGO

Brick-and-mortar refers to stores that sell their wares from a physical building. Online versions of those stores are sometimes called ***click-and-mortar***.

Many of your favorite brick-and-mortar stores, to whom you have been loyal over the years, now offer you the convenience of shopping online from their "click and mortar" stores. These tried and true stores are usually safe places to start.

You can also ask relatives and friends. Several good recommendations about an online store should increase the possibility that you will want to shop there.

Yet, sometimes you are faced with deciding if you want to make a purchase from a store with which you are completely unfamiliar. For instance, say you have been browsing for a while and you find a great buy on a cashmere sweater. You find your size and you like the color, but you've never heard of the company. Is it safe to buy this sweater online? What can you do to help ensure that your money and your privacy are protected? First of all, before you place your order, look for information about the company on its website, such as its mailing address (not just a post office box) and its telephone number.

Unfortunately, anyone can set up an Internet website. If you are unfamiliar with a particular company, one good way to check them out is to find out if they have a toll-free telephone number you can call to get more information about them. Again, ask your friends and neighbors if they are familiar with the company and ask for their feedback.

Sandy's tip

If you are completely unfamiliar with an online store, it is always smart to place a small order or two with them before you make a large purchase.

Secondly, read the site's privacy policy. Every reputable website that collects customer or user information should have a privacy policy explaining how they protect the information submitted to their website. Some online websites sell the information you give them to other companies. When making your purchase, be sure not to give them permission to share your information to other companies. Sometimes it's in the fine print, so be careful when you are placing your order. Exercise your right to opt out if you do not want the seller to pass along information about you. If you do not agree with their privacy policy, do not deal with that company.

There are several companies that put their seal of approval on privacy statements. This is kind of like having a Good Housekeeping seal of approval on a product. It certifies that the website adheres to strict privacy standards. TRUSTe, a nonprofit organization that promotes privacy on the Internet, is one of the most recognizable of these companies. If a website has a TRUSTe certification, it doesn't necessarily mean they carry good products or give good service, but it is an indication that they care about the customer and are more likely to be a substantial company.

Paying by Credit Card

After you have determined you are dealing with a reputable company, the most important thing to watch out for when making an online purchase is whether the web page on which you put your personal information, particularly your credit card number, is secure. There are several ways to confirm you are protected, so it is easy to practice safe online shopping.

There are two very simple ways to identify a web page as secure. Instead of the URL in the address bar beginning with http://, it begins with https://, the extra s stands for secure. See Figure 3.1 for an example.

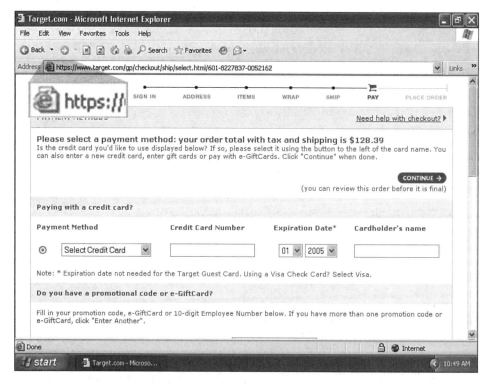

FIGURE 3.1

At the Target website you see the https:// in the address bar, indicating that you are on a secure web page.

In addition to seeing https://, you will also see a closed padlock, in all browsers. One is not present without the other. Both of these features represent secure sites that are using Secure Socket Layering (SSL), which is a particularly reliable encryption process that scrambles credit card information after it is entered and before it is transferred.

In Netscape and Opera, the lock is always visible, but it is in an unlocked state when the page is not secure. In Internet Explorer, look for a gold locked padlock at the bottom-right on the status bar. Firefox also puts a gold lock on the status bar, but it looks a bit different than the one in IE. Opera uses a gray lock to the right of the address bar, and Netscape Navigator uses a gold lock with a gold hue surrounding it on the status bar. Just remember that a closed lock, such as the one shown in Figure 3.2, means you are on a secure page.

Do not look for the entire site to be secure. The page on which you put your dress or shoe size, or where you indicated you want to purchase three copies of a certain book, does not need to be a secure page. However, do not do business with any company that does not offer you a secure page for your credit card, shipping, and billing information. Remember to look for the https:// and the closed padlock before entering any private personal information.

When you pay online using your credit card, the Fair Credit Billing Act will protect your transaction. Under this legislation, consumers have the right to dispute certain charges for goods or services they never received or ordered, and they may temporarily withhold their payment. Generally, customers are held liable for only the first $50 worth of unauthorized credit card charges. The type of credit card used, however, can make a difference. Some credit card companies provide supplemental warranties or other

Sandy's tip

Be careful with debit cards. Many do not have the Fair Credit Act protection, so you might be liable for more than $50 of unauthorized debit card charges. Check with your bank for details.

purchase-protection benefits. If you have a problem with your purchase, you might be able to withhold payment while your credit card company investigates the problem.

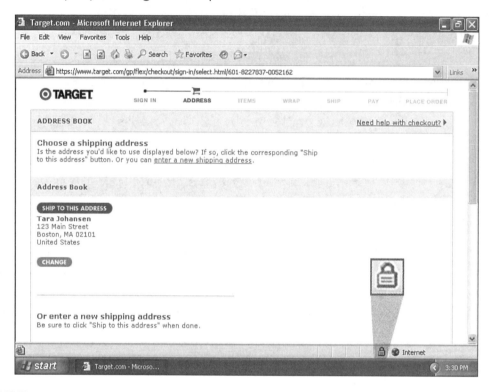

FIGURE 3.2
The closed yellow lock in the lower-right corner of this web page indicates that it is a secure page.

BLOOPER ALERT
Never enter your name, address, or credit card information until you have determined you are on a secure web page.

Check the Return Policy

When shopping online, do not place any orders until you thoroughly understand the company's return policy. What if you do not like what you purchased? Can it be returned? Is there a restocking fee? Will the company pay for the return postage if the product arrives damaged? If the website also has a brick-and-mortar store, can you return the product there? Will you get a refund or will you have to settle for a store credit? Even if you are dealing with a well-known business where you are a regular customer, be aware that some companies have different rules for their online shoppers than they do for purchasing items from their brick-and-mortar stores or mail order catalogs. You do not want any surprises, so do your homework. Most companies make this information easily understandable and accessible on their websites.

Shopping Carts and Shopping Fun

After you decide on a purchase, it is time to place the order. Many similarities exist among companies in the actual order process. For instance, most shopping sites allow you to use a virtual shopping cart. As you shop, you can add items to your cart, and when you have finished shopping, you can view the contents of your cart, remove any items you really do not want, and then complete your order. A favorite online bookseller is Amazon.com. It offers good prices, a large selection, excellent service, and free shipping on many items. Today Amazon.com sells everything from books to pet supplies. It's very easy to place an order with Amazon and the process is not unlike that of placing an order with most other online companies or catalogs.

You start out by going to Amazon.com's website at www.amazon.com. Then find what you want to purchase, add the item to your shopping cart, view your cart, and then place your order.

Let's go through the process of purchasing a current bestseller from Amazon.com in detail.

In your browser's address bar, type **www.amazon.com**. Press the Enter key on your keyboard to go to Amazon.com's website. Let's see what books Amazon.com has that you might be interested in purchasing. To do this, click the Books tab at the top of Amazon.com's home page, as shown in Figure 3.3.

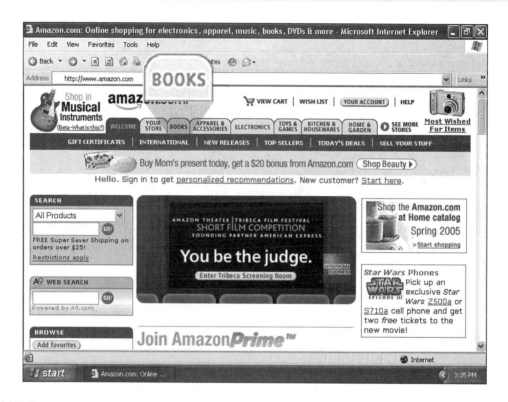

FIGURE 3.3
At Amazon.com, you choose what you want to search for by choosing a tab at the top of the screen.

At the next page, click the Bestsellers link as shown in Figure 3.4, and scroll through the list of bestsellers. When you find a book you are interested in, click the link (usually the title of the book) for the book to get more information about it. If you want to purchase this book, click the Add to Shopping Cart button.

Then continue shopping. When you get ready to check out, click the View Cart link. This link is at the top of the web page. You can review your order on your Shopping Cart page and you can remove items by clicking the Delete button. Or you can increase the quantity of an item by changing the Quantity number. Be sure to click the Update button to update the page if you make changes.

FIGURE 3.4
Narrow your Amazon.com search down by choosing the list of bestsellers.

When you are ready to check out, click the Proceed to Checkout button, as shown in Figure 3.5. Continue following the onscreen instructions until you have set up your free Amazon.com account. You will be prompted to fill in your shipping address, billing address, and other information. Each time you complete a portion of the form, click the Continue link. Remember to review every screen carefully and be sure the page that requests your credit card number is secure.

FIGURE 3.5
Amazon.com makes purchasing items easy.

The next time you visit the Amazon.com website, you will simply have to enter your username and password and Amazon.com will remember who you are. It will also remember your address and credit card information so that you won't have to enter it again. In fact, if you access Amazon.com from the same computer, it will probably recognize you immediately when you visit. Every time I visit Amazon.com, the top of the page says, "Hello, Sandy Berger."

Keep Good Records

When you have completed an online transaction, the last screen usually shows your order and confirmation number. Always print this page, just in case you have a problem with your purchase. You want to keep a written record of all shipping and handling costs, as well as the amount of the item(s).

Most companies will send you an email confirmation of your transaction. Be sure to read it as soon as you get it, particularly the fine print. By law, online businesses must deliver merchandise within 30 days of purchase or notify you if there will be a delay. It is not unusual for the company to send you additional email regarding your order. You might also get email correspondence telling you that your order has been filled and is ready to ship. You might even get a tracking number to use on the shipper's website to track the progress of the shipment.

It is a good idea to promptly check your monthly bank and credit card statements as soon as you are notified your order has been shipped. Reconcile these statements with the records of your transactions to make sure that any billing errors or unauthorized purchases are reported within the required timeframe.

Comparison Shopping

The real beauty of the Internet shines through when it helps you find the best price on any given item. You don't have to run from store to store. You don't even have to jump from website to website. You simply surf over to a comparison shopping website and let the website do the work of finding and comparing the prices on the item for which you are shopping.

Sandy's tip
Some comparison shopping sites allow the user to rate the store they purchased from, giving other visitors feedback on the quality of the online store.

For instance, I visited PriceGrabber to compare prices on a Canon PowerShot digital camera. The prices ranged from $157.97 to $239.99 and the website listed 54 online stores where it could be purchased. One nice feature of PriceGrabber and many other comparison websites is that after people purchase the item, they often return to the comparison site to write a review of the item. So when I visited just one website, I got 54 prices, 16 product reviews, a detailed description of the camera, and full specifications from the manufacturer. Some of these comparison sites will even watch the price of an item for you and notify you by email if the price comes down. Finding a bargain has never been easier! If you have never been to a comparison shopping site before, you will be amazed. These sites enable you to compare every thing from magazine subscriptions to automobiles.

LINGO

Comparison shopping sites are websites that will find and compare the prices of items from several competing online stores.

This list contains a few comparison shopping sites available online:

- **Shopping.com**—www.shopping.com
- **BizRate**—www.bizrate.com
- **Shopzilla**—www.shopzilla.com
- **PriceGrabber**—www.pricegrabber.com

Enhanced Product Presentations

Online retailers are always trying new ways to make their products appealing in an atmosphere where the customer doesn't have the option of feeling the merchandise or trying on the clothing. Television shopping programs have taken the lead in this area, probably because of their experience in selling in a "view only" atmosphere.

A quick look at the online versions of QVC, HSN (Home Shopping Network), Shop at Home TV, and ShopNBC, the top four television home shopping networks, reveals an extensive Internet presence.

All of these television merchants allow you to watch their live television programming through the Internet. On a dial-up connection, this type of television viewing is choppy and slow, but on a high-speed cable or DSL connection you can watch just as you would watch television. Not only do you get to see live TV, but the screen also shows information about the current item and, of course, provides a hot link for ordering the item. ShopatHomeTV.com even has online broadcasts of six archived programs so you can see what you might have missed on television.

QVC.com features more than 800,000 products, and the others are not far behind. The shopping channels have not only made it easy to comparison shop and purchase online, their websites have become community centers for their customers. There are online pictures and information on the show hosts, chat rooms, and bulletin boards.

The following is a list of four of the most popular shop-at-home sites:

- **QVC**—www.qvc.com

- **HSN**—www.hsn.com

- **ShopatHomeTV.com**—www.shopathometv.com

- **ShopNBC**—www.shopnbc.com

HSN.com has developed an interesting online tool to enhance its product presentation and make it easier to buy clothing. At its website you can create a virtual model. Enter your height, weight, and other statistics, and a model with your figure proportions will appear on the screen. You can even choose the hair color and style of your virtual model. Then you use your model to try on HSN clothing. You can try different outfits and even add shoes and accessories. You can rotate your model to see how she looks from all directions. HSN also has a stock model for you to use if you don't want to customize your own. You can get an idea of what the HSN virtual model looks like in Figure 3.6.

Lands' End at www.landsend.com has a virtual model for men as well as women. Now, guys, don't scoff at this. Try it out. You actually get a much better feel for how the clothing will look when you try it on the virtual model.

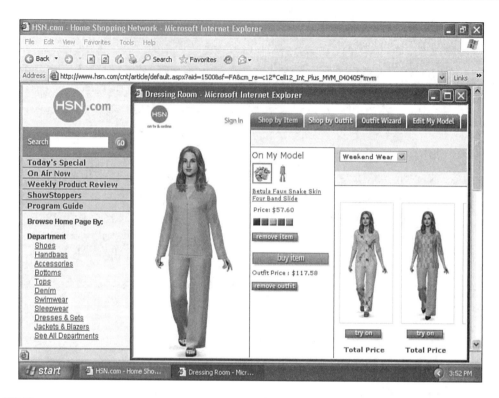

FIGURE 3.6
At HSN.com you can see how the clothes will look using a virtual model.

Other websites are using many different merchandising methods to attract purchasers. Shop for shoes at Nordstrom.com (www.nordstrom.com) and you will be able to zoom in and out to see all the details of the shoe. Many stores are offering the ability to click a button to see a larger view of the item. At some websites, such as J.Jill (www.jjill.com), you can see the item either on or off a model, and you can click on a color swatch to change the color of the item on the screen. At the Volkswagen website (www.vw.com) you can explore each car by a simple move of the mouse. You can change the color of the car and turn it around to see it from every angle.

Web shopping sites are finding that personalized product suggestions are helpful to the shopper and also sell more merchandise. When you shop for an item on QVC and many other websites, you are presented with other available items that are related to the product you are view-ing. You can either ignore these items or click on them for more infor-mation if you are interested. Amazon.com takes this idea one step further. Make a few purchases at Amazon.com, and the next time you visit, the site will suggest other items you might like to buy, based on your previous purchases. Quite often these product suggestions are accurate enough to be truly valuable.

Online Catalogs

What's the difference in purchasing mer-chandise from an online website, such as L.L.Bean (www.llbean.com), and purchas-ing from an online catalog? Actually, noth-ing. When you receive a catalog in the mail, if that company also has a website, which it very likely does, you can often purchase the same merchandise over its Internet site.

Sandy's tip
Some shopping websites have Web-only specials that aren't available at their physical stores or from their paper catalogs.

Some Internet retailers even re-create their paper catalogs online. You can flip through each page of the virtual cat-alog by clicking your mouse. These catalogs usually contain the exact pages you see in the paper catalog. For example, if you go to Coldwater Creek at www.coldwatercreek.com, you can access all of its mail order catalogs from its website (see Figure 3.7).

With Internet resources, you can search through catalogs even if you don't have the paper version. An easy way to access online catalogs is by going to CyberCatalogs at www.cybercatalogs.com. You can search for a particular catalog or you can look for an item and CyberCatalogs will get you a list of catalogs available that sell that product.

Google Catalogs is another popular database of mail-order catalogs. It is immense in size and represents everything kind of catalog you can imagine. Google not only gives you the full color catalogs in just a click or two, but it also provides a link to the vendor's website and the vendor's telephone number. If you want to check it out, go to http://catalogs.google.com.

FIGURE 3.7
At Coldwater Creek you can flip through the pages of its catalog using your mouse.

Customized Items

There is little doubt that computers and technology have already changed our lives. Consider bar codes, ATM machines, email, electronic tickets, and instant access to information, to name just a few. Yet, one of the biggest changes technology will make in our lives over the next few years might well be something that is just now making an appearance—personalization and customization.

Many products lend themselves to personalization. A good example is perfume. At a website call Eleuria, at www.eleuria.com, you can order a personalized fragrance, a service that was in the past was only available to blue bloods and the very wealthy. Prince Ranier had a perfume especially created for Grace Kelly as a wedding present. Now you can have the same luxurious experience by simply visiting a website and filling out a profile.

At the Nike website (www.nike.com), you can personalize your own gym shoes, hats, or other sports-related items. Not only can you choose the colors, but you can also include your own sayings and tags. Look around the Internet and you will find that you can add your own picture to mugs, mouse pads, calendars, photo cubes, or T-shirts. Sites such as the Kodak EasyShare Gallery (www. kodakgallery.com), Shutterfly (www. shutterfly.com), and Club Photo (www.clubphoto.com) specialize in these services. As a matter of fact, the variety of websites that are into personalization is almost mind-boggling. Websites such as Sweet Cravings at www.sweetcraving.com will take your logo, photo, or graphic and apply them to custom-created edible cookies in a variety of different shapes and sizes. Personal Creations at www.personalcreations.com will provide everything from personalized stationery to personalized furniture. There is even a Personalization Mall at www.personalizationmall.com where you can find twenty personalized gift stores.

Sandy's tip

Put your dog's picture on a mug, your husband's name on his golf balls, or the family photo on a canvas for framing. The Internet is the place to go for personalized presents.

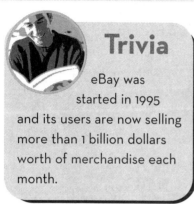

Trivia

eBay was started in 1995 and its users are now selling more than 1 billion dollars worth of merchandise each month.

Auctions and Used Stuff

What would a chapter on shopping be without a mention of one of the most popular Internet pastimes, online auctions? eBay, the granddaddy of them all, started in 1995 and has become one of the most recognizable and most used Internet services. Just about everything you can think of is available on eBay. It also has a few things you have probably never even thought of. Recent offerings include an old box of crayons, a lucky cowboy Ringo doll, a duct tape necktie, a drive-through restaurant, a ranch in New Mexico, and a hornet's nest.

Here's how it works. Assuming that everything has an inherent value, you can buy and sell just about any item, new or old, on eBay. There is no charge to visit eBay, look at the merchandise, or make a purchase. If you want to sell an item, there is a charge for listing that item on the website. You post a picture of the item and set a starting price. After it is listed, people bid on the item. You can also establish the price at which you will sell the item or you can just wait and see how high the bids go. After the bid has been accepted, the purchaser sends the money to the seller and the seller sends the item to the purchaser. The seller also pays eBay a fee for the sale. Not only is this a great way to get rid of the old stuff you are not using, it is an excellent way to find unusual items and to find some bargains. Thousands of people use eBay to buy and sell items to augment their income, and for some, it has become a full-time job. Others, like me, just visit to have some fun and to sell or bid on an occasional item.

With the popularity of eBay, many other auction websites have popped up. Even Amazon.com has an auction section in its website. Just type **online auctions** into any search engine and you will find enough auction sites to keep you busy for months.

If you are a real bargain hunter, try Freecycle at www.freecycle.org, where everything is free. This network of groups across the country allows you to "recycle" your unwanted items and lets you obtain free "treasures" from other people's junk. A truly unique shopping experience!

The Internet is also a fantastic resource for travel planning. You can buy airplane and train tickets from the comfort of your home. You can also book rental cars and hotels. See Chapter 4, "Easy Travel Planning," for more fantastic travel resources.

Disadvantages to Shopping Online

Shopping online has definite advantages and although it might sound like a dream come true, it has a few disadvantages as well. For instance, if you really want to purchase a gift for the birthday party you will be attending later today, you better warm up your car. Even with express service, online shopping does not offer instant delivery.

In addition, although the Internet can give you more information about a product you are considering, sometimes that information is not enough. On the Internet, you can read that a new perfume is a combination of gardenia, freesia, and sandalwood with a delicate top note of vanilla, but nothing can substitute for actually smelling the fragrance. Overall though, after you understand how to shop successfully and safely, you might be amazed at how much online shopping you will do.

Shopping online can be fun. If you are one of those shop-till-you-drop people, you can now choose where you want to drop—either in the mall parking lot, or at home in front of the computer.

Sandy's Summary

The Internet has put a whole new spin on shopping. Whether you are a shopaholic or you just purchase exactly what you need, online resources can save you time and money. You no longer have to "shop till you drop." Now you can shop in your robe and slippers using the Internet to make all your purchases.

Shopping online is safe and secure as long as you deal with a reputable company and learn how to recognize a secure web page when you enter your personal information. You will also want to investigate privacy and return policies.

After you do that, online shopping is just plain fun. You don't have to run from store to store to get prices. You can use comparison websites to find the best price on just about any item. You can flip through online catalogues with your mouse, try clothing on virtual models, and take advantage of Web-only special prices.

The Internet also specializes in personalized items. Put your pet's picture on a mug, buy perfume created just for you, or create gift baskets right from the comfort of your home. You'll feel like royalty.

With the Internet, you can even buy and sell used items. So clean out the garage or basement and make a few extra bucks without the hassle of a garage sale. Then you can go online and find that treasure you have been longing for.

Shop online. It's fun and easy!

Sandy Berger

Chapter 4

Easy Travel Planning

The world is a book, and those who do not travel read only a page.
—Saint Augustine

Travel planning often involves a lot of time and aggravation. Technology, however, goes a long way to reduce it. The Internet enables you to plan your trips and routes, compare prices, book online, and print your boarding pass—all from home. You can even visit the world without leaving home through the wonders found on your computer and the Internet.

Travel Planning Internet Resources

Today baby boomers are retiring earlier than their parents did. Even if you have not yet retired, you, along with thousands of other Americans, are on the highways, in trains, and

IN THIS CHAPTER

- Travel Discounts
- Global Positioning Systems
- Armchair Travel
- Pet Travel

aboard planes traveling to your dream vacation destinations. Armed with more disposable income, more leisure time, and a longer life span, today's boomers and zoomers are giving in to their wanderlust and following their spirit of adventure.

Trivia

Technology has made great strides in the air. The wingspan of the Boeing 747 is longer than the Wright brothers' first flight.

The largest phenomenon affecting the increased popularity in travel is the Internet. The World Wide Web now provides travel information and e-tickets for any traveler with access to the Internet. In the past, travel agencies and airlines had a monopoly on ticket sales, but now thanks to online communications, any adult with a credit card and access to the Internet can make all his travel plans and reservations online. Internet resources make it easy to shop for flights, book hotel rooms, and rent cars. In short, the Internet makes travel planning easier and makes travel dollars go farther.

Finding a reliable travel site is as easy as pie but determining which one to use can be a tough decision. Two excellent websites that offer extensive travel services are Travelocity (www.travelocity.com, see Figure 4.1) and Microsoft's Expedia (www.expedia.com).

Orbitz (www.orbitz.com), originally founded by American, United, Northwest, Delta, and Continental Airlines, is another very popular trip-planning site. Each of these services allows you to shop for vacations, book flights, reserve hotel rooms, and rent cars. They each have special deals and personalized features. You will be expected to register at all of these sites, but registration is free.

A Word to the Wise

The world of travel and online booking, like everything else, has its pitfalls. Remember these words to the wise. Don't be blinded by an attractive fare. Check to make sure there are no surcharges, fuel charges, or special fees. This is especially true when traveling abroad. Advertised rates of airfares do not always include the extra tariffs that impact

international fares. These extra costs can include hefty taxes and government fees. To be fully prepared, look for information on extra
charges ahead of time. It is always advisable to check to see if these
fees have to be paid in cash.

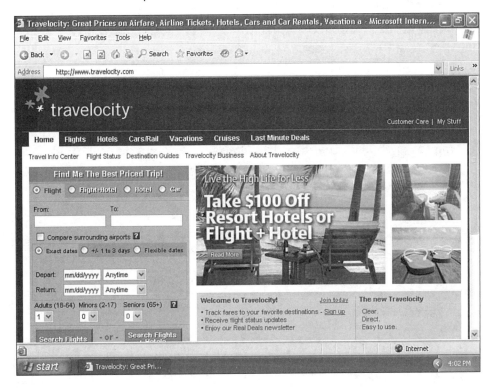

FIGURE 4.1
Travelocity is just one of the many websites you can use to help you plan your travel.

If you are buying a bargain package over the Internet, be careful. Your
dream vacation can become a nightmare if you fall victim to a travel
scam. Although many travel opportunities are legitimate, scam opera-
tors defraud millions of dollars from travelers each year. Be wary of bargains that require you to purchase add-ons that are more expensive.
Check out the services and accommodations in advance to avoid paying for nonexistent services or accommodations in unsafe or less-than-
desirable locations. It's a good idea to thoroughly investigate a travel

website before you purchase anything. Ask friends and relatives which sites they have used successfully before you buy.

Travel Bargains and Discounts

The Internet offers convenience as well as bargains. There are several websites that do travel comparison and research work for you by scouring the Web for the lowest fares. Yahoo!'s FareChase site, at www.farechase.com, and SideStep, at www.sidestep.com, are gaining in popularity by offering a one-stop location that searches various e-ticket sites for the traveler. FareChase and SideStep help you save time and money by pulling together the Web's best travel deals in one place for airline fares, car rental, and hotels. Other comparison travel sites include Booking Buddy at www.bookingbuddy.com, Cheapfares at www.cheapfares.com (see Figure 4.2), and TripMania at www.tripmania.com.

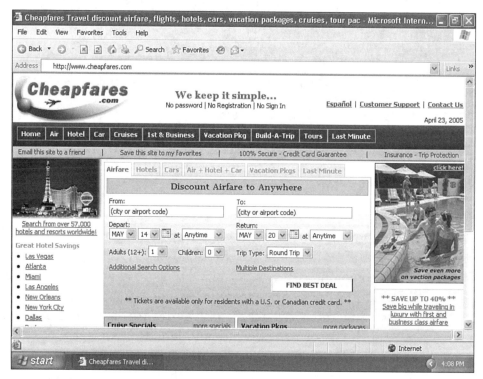

FIGURE 4.2
Visit Cheapfares.com and other comparison travel sites to find travel bargains.

Many of the comparison shopping websites we discussed in Chapter 2, "Search and Learn Online," also offer comparisons on airline tickets, vacation packages, car rentals, cruises, hotels, and other travel services. So be sure to check out Shopzilla (www.shopzilla.com), Shopping.com (www.shopping.com), and other comparison shopping sites.

For travel by train, Amtrak offers travelers 62 and over discounts on train fares. Certain cruise ships shave hundreds of dollars off the price of selected cruises for travelers 55 and over. Search carefully so you will discover these special discounts.

Sandy's tip

Most airlines now allow you to print your boarding pass at home. In most cases, you can check your bags with a skycap at the curb or use a kiosk inside to check your bags, completely avoiding long check-in lines.

Email Notice

Other ways to take advantage of these great travel offerings is to register online at an airline's website. Airline companies use email releases to announce many of their special fares. After you have registered, you can complete an online form indicating your departure date and destination city. The airline will email you a listing of fares as they become available.

For example, United Airlines sends out a weekly newsletter that lists special deals for weekend travel in the domestic United States. As is usual with any airlines, some restrictions might apply, but the fares are often quite worthwhile. The E-Fares list displays the departure city, destination city, and price. Visit the United website at www.united.com and click on the Deals link. This provides an easy way to view all of United's bargains in one place. Locations and fares change

BLOOPER ALERT

Although many travel sites compare rates, you don't have to deal with only one website. It is always advisable to compare the comparison sites. Visit several. Each will have different information and a unique way to present the information.

every week and many are available only online. Most other prominent airlines, such as American, Delta, Southwest, and US Airways, have similar services.

Discount Traveling for Boomers and Zoomers

Some younger travelers look at us enviously because the growing group of boomer and zoomer travelers often seem to get the best deals. The travel industry recognizes this group with many standard discounts. Unfortunately, many still use the antiquated word *senior* to indicate the recipients of these fares. Yet there are those who are spicing up even the nomenclature. Kudos to United Airlines for offering special savings for those over 55, called *Silver Wings Plus*.

Sandy's tip
Always put your name and address on both the inside and outside of all suitcases and travel bags. If you already have this information on your luggage, make sure the address is current.

BLOOPER ALERT
If the price seems too good to be true, it probably is. Check all bargain travel fares for hidden surcharges and additional fees.

When planning your trip, be sure to look for other special bargains. Discounts are sometimes offered for grandparents flying with grandchildren. Check out discounts for travel offered by organizations such as AARP. At its Travel area at www.aarp.org/travel, you can subscribe to the online AARP Travel Newsletter and stay in the know about members-only travel deals.

Several airlines offer a standard 10% discount for "seniors." The age that this kicks in at differs from airline to airline. If you meet the age requirement, in many cases you can get even more than the 10% discount. There are many special discounts for those over a certain age in addition to or instead of the standard discounts.

According to Tom Parsons of Best Fares (www.bestfares.com), senior fares are hidden fares, typically anywhere from 50% to 70% cheaper than the lowest regular fare. He claims these fares are available in 80% of the market. Tom encourages older Americans to look specifically for the special fares instead of the usual 10% discount for those over 60. Many major hotel chains also have special prices that save up to 50%, but you must ask. Again the age requirement for these preferred prices varies from hotel to hotel.

Technology in the Air

In April 2003, Delta Air Lines announced a new airline named Song. Its main travel routes are between the northeastern United States and Florida, but the impact of Song sent waves across the entire airline industry. While following other airlines by charging for amenities such as in-flight meals, Song decided to take a different route in its decision to offer technology-enhanced flights. It unveiled the world's most sophisticated in-flight entertainment technology among single aisle aircraft. Song collaborated with Matsushita Avionics Systems Corporation (MAS) and EchoStar Communications Corporation's DISH Network satellite TV to provide a comprehensive network of onboard entertainment amenities. Each seat has live satellite television, pay-per-view movie programming, MP3 audio programming, and interactive video games.

While Song is making a splash in the in-flight entertainment business, other airlines are now implementing in-flight Internet access. Even though the airlines struggle for profitability, technology cannot be denied its place in the air.

Last Minute Travel

In the travel industry, it is never too late to book a bargain ticket. In certain cases, a round-trip ticket to a vacation destination might be offered for as little as 25% of the usual costs, as an attempt to fill

Sandy's tip

When traveling, always take a statement from your physician detailing any particular problems or allergies. It is also advisable to take a copy of medication and eyeglass prescriptions. Carry necessary medications with you rather than putting them in checked luggage.

Sandy's tip

On most airlines, making a flight reservation and purchasing a ticket are two separate functions. Making a reservation confirms a seat on a particular flight. The actual fare is not locked in until you actually purchase the ticket.

unsold seats on the plane. The same is true of hotel reservations.

Who can take better advantage of this immediacy than boomer and zoomer travelers? Retired zoomers who have fewer job and family constraints can often make their own schedule and have the freedom to take advantage of last minute discounts. Boomers and zoomers who are still working often have more vacation time than their younger counterparts and might have the flexibility to book the cheaper roundtrip flights that have unusual requirements such as traveling only on a Tuesday or Thursday.

Maps and Global Positioning Systems

Being directionally impaired, I am well practiced at refolding that big old paper map. However, getting it back to its neat original size was a talent I never seemed able to develop. How well I remember the painful process of looking for a little town in Ohio by unfolding the entire map, finding the index printed in miniscule type, and then trying to locate C9. Thank goodness computers and technology have taken us away from those "good old days."

LINGO

GPS stands for Global Positioning System. This is a navigation system formed by 24 satellites orbiting the earth that are able to read the exact location of a GPS receiver.

Today, whether you are traveling across town or across the nation, you can use high-tech tools to help you find your way. Free mapping websites will plot your route. Global Positioning Systems (GPS) locate you by satellite and give you directions to your destination. Software mapping programs will figure your mileage, gas cost, and customize your route.

Mapping Websites

Mapping websites allow you to print maps as well as plan your route. Internet maps are generally more up-to-date than those old paper maps because the Internet is updated so frequently. The best part about these mapping sites is that the information is free.

The most well-known map site can be found at www.mapquest.com. MapQuest's website boasts that it is "the leader in helping consumers find anyplace in the physical world over any connected device" and is ranked within the top 10 most powerful U.S. brands on the Internet by NetRatings. Mapquest.com accommodates more than 37 million visitors every month.

If you are looking for a certain business or perhaps a business category, such as Hilton Hotels in the Washington, D.C. area, you can use Mapquest's Find It feature to get information on the business or to view a list of businesses related to the category you searched for. Find It provides you with an interactive map, as well as point-by-point driving directions (see Figure 4.3).

If what you are interested in is getting a map of some area of the world, Mapquest's Map feature is an excellent resource. It allows you to view detailed maps of approximately 250 countries or regions around the world, as well as nearly every conceivable city and town in America, including the Virgin Islands.

Perhaps the most popular feature of Mapquest is its Driving Directions. While you can also get directions by using the Find It feature, this special feature allows you to concentrate specifically on how to drive from point A to point B and then on to point C and back home again. You can get a reverse route to make getting home easier and the printed directions not only show how many miles you will travel on each leg of your trip, but also show you what the road and directional signs look like. You are provided with how long your trip will take and how many miles you will travel. Mapquest also allows you to search for driving directions in about a dozen European countries, including France, Germany, Luxemburg, and Spain.

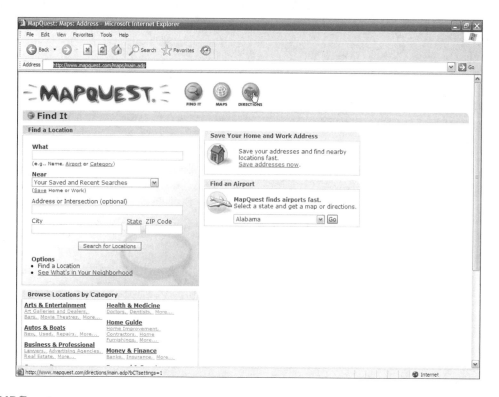

FIGURE 4.3
Mapquest's Find It feature will help you even if you don't know the exact address.

Yahoo! and Google, two websites traditionally known as search engines, are now providing extensive maps as well. For a quick map, you can simply type an address into the Yahoo! search engine at www.yahoo.com. For more advanced options, go directly to http://maps.yahoo.com. Yahoo! Maps gives you turn-by-turn driving directions as well as printed directions. One feature called SmartView offers an interactive and visual way for consumers to search for local content on the Web.

SmartView, as shown in Figure 4.4, allows you to choose local points of interest and attractions, such as restaurants or hotels, movie theaters, parks, and even ATMs and post offices in order to customize the current map displayed on your screen.

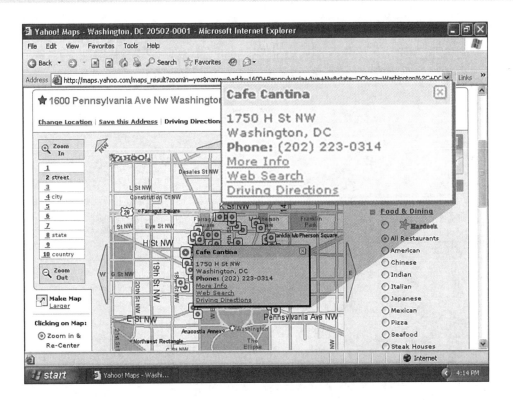

FIGURE 4.4
The SmartView option in Yahoo! is useful for finding hotels, restaurants, and other local amenities.

To use SmartView at Yahoo! Maps, you simply type in your location, and then use the SmartView Menu to find what you are looking for. Choose food and dining, recreation, shopping, gas stations, and hotels. You can even find the nearby wireless hot spots.

Just for fun, I typed in the address of the White House on Google Maps. The map showing 1600 Pennsylvania Avenue is shown in Figure 4.5.

Would you like to view your home from a satellite? Just type your address into Google Maps at http://maps.google.com. You will see a map of the area where you live and have the capability to zoom in and out and pan up and down. Click on the word *satellite* and there it is—a satellite image of your neighborhood. I put in the address of the White

House into the satellite view at Google Maps. You can see the results in Figure 4.6. It looks quite different than the map view in Figure 4.5.

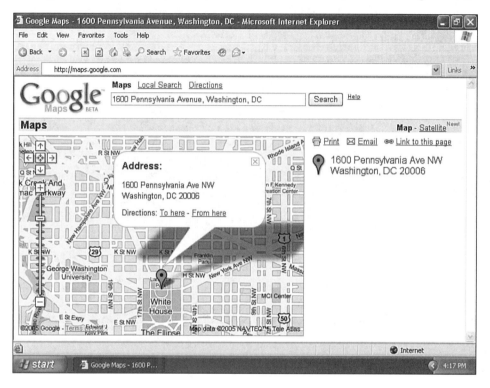

FIGURE 4.5
Google Maps shows 1600 Pennsylvania Avenue NW, Washington, D.C on a map.

Global Positioning Systems

The Global Positioning System (GPS) device utilizes satellite technology to pinpoint an exact location anywhere on the planet. Some GPS devices have their own built-in maps, compasses, and even voice navigation. These navigation systems are becoming a popular option in automobiles. The driver simply enters the location of her destination. The GPS device determines the best route and displays it on the screen. The best part is that the device then locates your current position and gives you voice commands, telling you exactly where and which way to turn and how far to travel to your destination. With a GPS system, women no longer have to stop at the gas station for directions and men no longer have to drive around pretending that they don't need to stop and ask for directions.

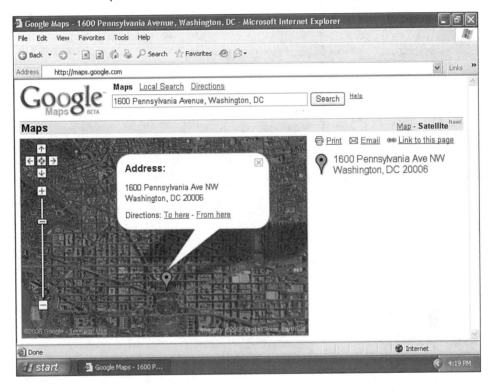

FIGURE 4.6
Google Maps shows a satellite image of 1600 Pennsylvania Avenue NW, Washington, D.C.

OnStar is one GPS device and service that is optional on most new GM automobiles. Handheld GPS devices are also available for those who don't have a GPS permanently installed in their cars.

Besides navigation in cars, GPS systems are used for some serious tasks, including navigation for military forces, forestry,

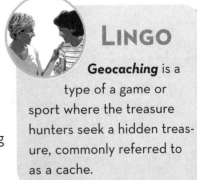

LINGO

Geocaching is a type of a game or sport where the treasure hunters seek a hidden treasure, commonly referred to as a cache.

Sandy's tip

GPS systems in today's automobiles vary greatly. If you want to get a GPS system on your new car, be sure to try out all the functions before you make your purchase. Remember that most have a monthly service fee attached.

mineral exploration, and wildlife habitation management. GPS units have also spawned an interesting new hobby called geocaching. If you liked going on treasure hunts when you were a kid, you will love this new high-tech form of this popular old game. People hide the treasure, called a cache, and then they post the location of the cache on the Internet. Treasure hunters use a handheld GPS system to find the treasure that can be anything from a comic book to jelly beans to real money. This new sport is becoming especially popular with vacationers and travelers because caches are hidden all over the world.

Mapping Programs

Although you can get free maps on the Internet, having a mapping program on your computer means you will have access to your maps even when you are offline. These mapping programs also have features that are not found on mapping websites. One example is the Microsoft Streets & Trips program.

LINGO

A **PDA** is a handheld device that acts as a minicomputer. A PDA functions as a personal organizer and usually contains appointments, to-do lists, and contact information for friends and associates. One major advantage of using PDAs is their ability to synchronize data with desktop and laptop computers.

Streets & Trips 2005 comes with an optional GPS locator. This popular program has always been a good mapping program, but the addition of a GPS system makes this product even better. The software is installed on your computer and gives you a detailed route map and driving instructions. It includes points of interest, restaurants, gas stations, and ATMs. Just enter in your starting point and your destination and you are given detailed directions. Add other information such as your gas mileage and the program will spit out gasoline costs and other pertinent information, and you can customize your trip to suit your needs.

Take Streets & Trips along for the ride on a laptop computer or PDA. Plug the small global positioning unit into your portable device and use the included suction cup to place the GPS apparatus on the car window. A small car appears on the computer screen indicating exactly where you are located and the progress of your trip. If you make a wrong turn, the program recalculates your route automatically. Almost any GPS device will work with Streets & Trips and you can purchase the program with or without the GPS unit. The included GPS component has no added fees or monthly charges. For car trips, it works best with two or more people: one to drive and one to navigate. It is a great new use for today's technology and it will be a useful tool for many travelers.

Armchair Travel

Without a doubt, travel and sightseeing are fun and enriching experiences, yet travel takes a lot of time, money, and energy. If you are short of cash or pressed for time, why not stay at home with your computer and do a little armchair traveling? You can have an incredible experience by taking your dream vacation online. The Web allows you to do more than just look at pictures in travel brochures. You can take a virtual tour around the world and experience real-time events taking place on street corners or in harbors, and also enjoy many other unique venues via the Internet.

Today many Internet sites use webcams to capture happenings in locales around the world. A webcam is a digital camera that records live action and transfers it to the Internet. Webcams allow you to view real-time activities.

To give you an example of what webcams are all about, visit a website called Around the World in 80 Clicks. It can be found at www.steveweb.com/80clicks, as

Sandy's tip
A simple Internet search for webcams will lead to you places where you can view everything from skiers in the Alps to sun-lovers at the beach.

shown in Figure 4.7. The tour starts in New York and continues to Canada, Ireland, France, Monaco, Denmark, Poland, Finland, Peru, and 71 other great sites around the world. Each stop is unique. You might see a live camera showing activities at the Eiffel Tower, a casino in Monte Carlo, or a street corner in Montreal. Sometimes the information is given in the local language, adding an even more foreign flare to the experience. Because pictures are worth a thousand words, it's never boring.

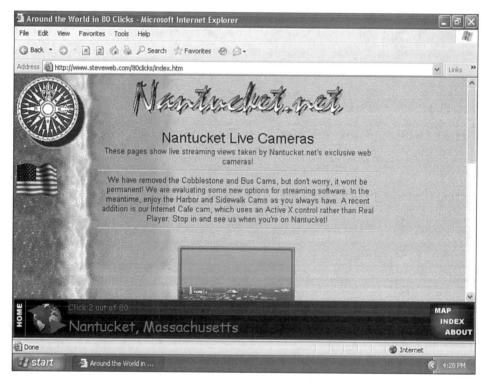

FIGURE 4.7
Around the World in 80 Clicks is a website that enables you to take a virtual tour of the world.

Everyone has heard of the Taj Mahal, but not everyone knows what it looks like or even where it is located. Why not make that your first stop? The Taj Mahal virtual tour can be found at www.taj-mahal.net. This website uses a web browser plug-in called QuickTime to display this world-famous landmark in detail. If you don't already have

QuickTime installed, you will be asked to download it free. QuickTime allows you to use directional arrows to pan across the vistas of the Taj Mahal. You can also click on the icon in the middle of the screen and drag it in any direction to get a complete 360° viewing of the palace and surrounding grounds. You can use the same technology to view interior vistas as you explore the many rooms of the royal residence.

LINGO

A *plug-in* is a small piece of software that adds features to a larger piece of software. Internet browsers often use plug-ins to increase the functionality of the basic program.

The well-known and much-loved Louvre Museum in Paris, France also has a wonderful virtual web tour. Like the Taj Mahal, the Louvre uses the QuickTime mechanism to show you around. Visit the Louvre's website at www.louvre.fr/louvrea.htm and click on Virtual Tours. You can peruse the painting and drawing galleries, the sculptures, and so much more—all with realistic views that make you feel like you are really there. Be sure to click on the architectural views to experience the impressive glass pyramid of the Louvre at night. It is spectacular.

With websites and technology getting better and better, we do not have to leave our homes to get a real feel for what the rest of the world is all about. If you surf around the Web a little, you are sure to find more exciting websites like the ones mentioned here. Let the Internet's webcams and virtual tours be your ticket to armchair enjoyment. All aboard!

Rovin' With Rover

As a pet owner you might be forced to bring your darlings along when moving great distances. Or you might feel that you just can't leave Rover behind when you take that long-awaited family vacation. Traveling with pets can be a pleasant experience for both you and your pet—if you plan ahead. There are even vacations and tours created specifically for adventuresome pet owners and their creature companions. If you

Sandy's tip
    If you have a pet
and you love to
travel, the Internet can
give you travel tips and will
also help you find places
to stay.

have Rover or Kitty at your side for the journey, your computer and the Internet can make your trip run more smoothly.

Dog might be man's best friend, but when it comes to rovin' with Rover, the Internet is sure to be your next best friend. Using the Internet for research and planning before your trip can assure that your vacation is pleasurable and relaxing. Websites for traveling with pets are abundant and informative. You'll find free directories for lost pets, information on lodging, as well as airline travel requirements and more.

In my recent flights I have been somewhat amazed by the number of pets that board the plane with their owners. There seems to be an abundance of soft, airline-approved, carry-on kennels called Sherpa Bags going through the security checks and onto planes. Small pets can be transported in the passenger cabin as carry-on luggage as long as the container will fit under the seat. Some airlines charge up to $50 extra to accommodate pets, even in a kennel under the seat.

Trivia

    Looking for a
    record to break?
The Guinness Book of
World Records says that
Edwin Shackleton has flown
in a total of 806 types of
aircraft.

If your pet is larger and has to travel on the airline, you will need to arrange for an approved crate. These crates are available for dogs from 2 pounds to 200 pounds. Many airlines also charge a fee, typically about $75, to check animals in cargo holds. A certificate of health is almost always required, even for domestic travel. So be sure to contact the airline beforehand to make the necessary arrangements.

Note there is often a variance in rules from airline to airline and even from month to month. In May of 2000, Delta Airlines, United Airlines, and American Airlines discontinued checking pets as baggage during the summer months because of the dangerous heat in the cramped cargo holds. A good rule of thumb is to avoid flying with pets when temperatures are less than 40° or more than 80° at either your departure city or destination.

Pet Travel Safety

When you load the family (including Rover and Kitty) in the minivan heading to Florida for a week of sun and fun, advance planning can be the difference between a delightful vacation and a disastrous one. The Internet is a bountiful source for your travel planning.

Most Internet sites advise keeping your animal contained with a pet seatbelt or secured carrier. Doggie car harnesses are specially designed with an extra loop to be used with the standard seatbelt. Containing your pet serves several purposes. In case of an accident, your pet is not thrown about the car, and a restraint also prevents the animal from causing an accident by jumping into the driver's lap or line of vision. A restraint also prevents the pet from getting loose when the door is opened.

Other sites on the Internethelp you find medical insurance and ID tags for your pets and allow you to look up information on veterinarians in the area of your destination. A convenient checklist is offered for pets traveling by car at Traveling with Pets (http://seniors-site.com/travel/pets.html).

Pet-Friendly Accommodations

Did you know that there are more than 25,000 hotels, inns, campgrounds, ranches, and resorts that welcome pets? If you are traveling more than a day's ride, you might need to find one of these accommodation sites that accept pets. Again, vacationing with pets can be rewarding if you take the time to do some research in advance. If you want your pet to stay in your room with you, the following are some questions to ask when making your reservations:

- Do you accept pets?
- Are there any pet fees or deposits?
- Are the fees per pet or per room?
- Are the fees charged daily or per visit?
- Is the deposit refundable?

- Are pets limited to certain types of rooms?

- Are there any areas I can't go into with my pet?

- Do you offer anything special for pets?

Some places cater to pets, offering pet sitting, walking, welcome gifts, and even room service items. Remember that policies change often. The hotel you stayed in last year might not allow pets this year.

The Internet has some great sites that have done most of the work for you. Simply visit these sites and get the answers to the above questions. The Pet Travel and Leisure site at www.pettravelleisure.com offers a pet travel guide that covers everything from quaint bed and breakfasts that welcome pets, five-star hotels that provide pet sitting while you shop, parks and beaches that allow you to bring your dog, and even restaurants that allow you to dine with your cat or dog.

The most extensive site is Pets Welcome at www.petswelcome.com with its listings page for thousands of pet-friendly hotels, B&Bs, ski resorts, campgrounds, and beaches (see Figure 4.8). Its Travel Info section gives information on how to take your pet anywhere. You can get information on pertinent pet travel, a boarding kennel database, emergency info, pet sitters, and advice on air travel.

Another free online directory to pet-friendly hotels worldwide is available at Travel Pets (www.travelpets.com), with featured bed and breakfast accommodations plus great links to other pet-oriented locations. Get instant access to pet-friendly lodging in the United States, including vacation rentals, cabins, inns, condos, cottages, resorts, and lodges at Pet Friendly Travel (www.petfriendlytravel.com). Listings are by state. Many of these sites provide links to the country's major airlines with information on pets.

So no matter if Rover or Kitty are by your side when you are flying overseas or headed to the state park to spend some time with your "best friend," both you and your pet will have a better experience if you have planned ahead. Why not let the Internet be the new trick you learn for your old (or new) dog?

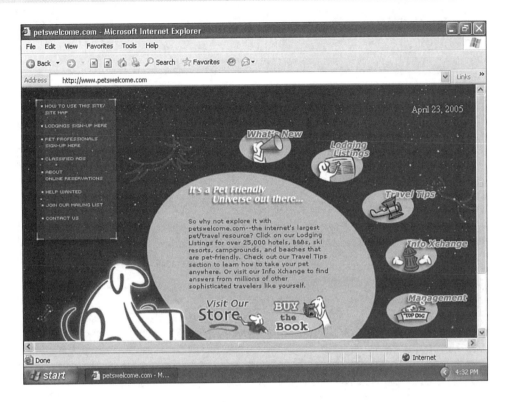

FIGURE 4.8
The Pets Welcome website will help you find everything from pet-friendly beaches to emergency veterinarians.

On the Road

Many boomers and zoomers are fulfilling their lifelong dream of taking to the road. Traveling in cars or RVs, these explorers might choose a short trip or they might be on the road for months at a time. The Internet is a valuable resource for them with information on RV parks, hotels, and motels. One popular website is RV Travel

Trivia

The original Route 66 spanned 2,000 miles through Illinois, Missouri, Kansas, Oklahoma, Texas, New Mexico, Arizona, and California. Visiting the remaining stretches of Route 66 has become a popular pastime as visitors see where the chrome meets the road.

(www.rvtravel.com) with news, information and travel advice for RVers. If you travel in an RV, you will also want to check out FunRoads.com at www.funroads.com, where you can get weather forecasts, maps, estimated driving times, and a round up of some of the country's favorite RVing destinations (see Figure 4.9).

FIGURE 4.9
The FunRoads.com website has a wealth of information for RVers.

Because many travelers carry a laptop computer for information and communications, wireless hotspots have become very popular. RV Travel has a list of hotspots. You can also find a hotspot at the Wi-FiHotSpotList.com website at www.wi-fihotspotlist.com.

Whether by plane, train, automobile, or RV, boomers and zoomers are traveling more and using the Internet and high-tech resources to aid their travels. Their motto is "Be wise and be mobile." They know there will be plenty of time for that rocking chair... later.

LINGO

Hotspots are places that provide public wireless broadband Internet services. Airports, train stations, libraries, hotels, and even parks can be Internet hotspots.

Sandy's Summary

Many of us have dreamed of traveling to other states and even to foreign lands. As we get older, we often decide that we have put off traveling too long. Now is the time! Whether you want to go across the state or around the world, technology can help cut through much of the aggravation of planning a trip.

If going by air, websites of airlines and hotels will help you create the expedition you've dreamed of. You'll save money by using comparison travel sites. You can avoid long lines at the airport by getting your boarding pass online and checking your bags at curbside. You will also save money by looking for special fares targeted at boomers and zoomers.

When traveling by car, RV, or even by foot, the new global positioning systems (GPS) will help you find your way. Mapping software and websites will make sure you don't have to stop to ask for directions.

If health or financial restraints limit your travel, don't worry. With webcams you see the entire world without ever leaving home.

The Internet will also help you when you are rovin' with Rover or Kitty. There are tons of websites to help you find appropriate places to stay and to visit with your animal friends. RVers will love Internet resources to find new trends, fast roads, and comfortable places to park overnight.

You don't want to be without email and the Internet when you travel. Check the Internet before you leave for lists of hotspots where you can use your wireless laptop. If you plan your whole trip around these hotspots, you'll never be out of touch.

Using these wonderful high-tech resources you'll be smiling as you sing along with Willie Nelson as he croons, "On the road again. Just can't wait to get on the road again."

Sandy Berger

Chapter 5

Managing Your Finances

"The pen is mightier than the sword, but no match for the accountant."
—Jonathan Glancey

*E*ach chapter in this book demonstrates how today's technological advances can enhance just about every aspect of your life. They can even make the most tedious tasks easier. This is especially true when dealing with managing your finances. Long gone are the days of idling in long lines at the bank. Waiting for checks to clear—not anymore. Think investing in the stock market is exclusive to major brokers—think again! Your computer and the Internet can help you manage your finances more quickly and easily than ever before.

Personal Finance Software

One of the best ways to get control of your money and to make financial tasks easier is to computerize your financial data. In order to do this you will need a software application that offers you all of the options and tools to fit your needs. Some applications give you just a basic checkbook register and tools to manage accounts as well as run reports and create budgets. Other types of software can be used to keep track of the finances of a small business. No matter where in the spectrum you are, there is a solution for you.

Choosing the Software

The two most popular financial software programs are Microsoft Money (www.microsoft.com/money) and Intuit's Quicken (www.quicken.com). I am partial to Quicken because I have used it since its first version in 1993 and it is also available for the Mac. Money is a newer program (nothing wrong with that), but it is a Windows-only program.

Quicken and Money are both good programs. They seem to leap frog each other with each new version. So one year Quicken might have slightly better features. The next year the program with the best features might be Money. If you received either Money or Quicken with your computer, just go ahead and use that. If you use accountants to do your taxes, you might want to find out if they have a financial program they would like you to use. Also check with your bank to see which program they support if you are interested in using online banking.

Both Quicken and Money have various versions from which to choose. They might be called Standard, Deluxe, Premium, Premiere, or the like. The easiest way to decide which version you need is to go to the Money or Quicken websites where each has a list of products and how they compare. Money also has a Small Business edition. The business version of Quicken is called QuickBooks.

You can find more information on these financial products by going to their respective websites:

- **Microsoft Money**—www.microsoft.com/money/default.mspx

Sandy's tip

Don't buy Quicken or Money at the retail prices. Warehouse stores, such as Costco and Sam's, and many online stores offer discounts.

- **Intuit's Quicken**—www.quicken.com
- **Intuit's QuickBooks**—www.quickbooks.com

Features and Tools Found in Finance Software

These financial programs automate all of your everyday economic tasks. They can track your checks and balance your checkbook. If you have been accurate at documenting the checks as you write them, the reconciliation is usually right on track. It is really exciting the first time to see all that tedious work done for you with the press of a mouse button. Check with your bank. If its online banking is compatible with the software program you are using, you can download your monthly bank statement right into your check register within the program. You will still have to check each transaction, but many people use this feature, especially if they pay most of their bills online.

Financial programs, such as Quicken and Money, allow you to budget your money and track your spending, categorize your payments, pay bills online right from within the program, accumulate items for taxes, and even schedule payments in advance. They have excellent reporting capabilities. Some versions also help you monitor your mutual funds and stock purchases, build a retirement plan, and perform tax planning.

Don't shy away from these programs. They are easy to set up and easy to use. You will invest some time inputting data, but computerizing your finances is well worth the effort.

Other financial software programs are available for alternative tasks. Intuit also has programs, such as Quicken Medical Expense Manager and Quicken Rental

BLOOPER ALERT

After you set up your checkbook on the computer, you need to keep your check entry up-to-date. Many people leave this to the end of the month when it becomes a bigger chore than necessary. Be sure to enter checks, cash withdrawals, and debit transactions as they occur.

Sandy's tip
Back up your financial data regularly. Both Quicken and Money allow you to make a backup right from within the program. Save that backup to an external drive, CD, or DVD occasionally to provide you with a restore point should you ever lose data on your computer.

Sandy's tip
When selecting an online bank, it is best to use a traditional bank that you know and trust. In choosing any online bank, make sure it is legitimate and that your deposits are federally insured.

Property Manager, to assist with specific financial tracking. Although they are more difficult to set up than dedicated financial programs, you can use spreadsheet programs, such as Microsoft Excel, to create your own financial tracking worksheets (if you are a do-it-yourself person) .

Online Banking and Bill Paying

If you have a standard checking or savings account, chances are that you already have the option of managing your account online. In fact, most major banks allow all the power of Internet transactions at no extra cost to you! The advantages of managing your account(s) online are many:

- Pay bills online

- Track purchases

- Keep tabs on deposits and deductions

- Automatic bill payments

- View returned checks

- Transfer funds from one account to another instantly

Enrolling is easy. Simply ask a representative at your local branch, call your bank's toll-free service line (typically on the back of your ATM card), or visit its homepage to start enjoying the freedom of virtual banking. Just think how nice it would be to eliminate that grueling task of balancing your checkbook. If you are still concerned about breaking out of your money-mold, here are some positives you can expect after making the transition:

- Eliminate visits to your local bank

- No waiting in teller lines

- Faster, more accurate transactions
- Do your banking anytime day or night
- Save money on stamps and envelopes
- Pay bills on their due date not having to leave 3–5 days for the mail to go through

Most banks now have an online bill-paying service that is included with your online banking, usually at no extra cost. Many also have online tutorials that will show you exactly how to set up the online bill-paying service. There is a once-only time investment needed here to set up the accounts, but you will save much time and effort in the long run. You can also pay bills online by using the website of the vendor, who then debits your checking account. You can ease into online banking by doing one or two transactions a month. After you see the ease of use, you are sure to want to do more.

> **Sandy's tip**
> If you arrange for automatic bill paying from your checking account, be sure to read the fine print. Depending on the bank the money might be withdrawn before the due date. It is important to know exactly when the funds will be transferred.

Security

Don't be afraid of online banking. There are now millions of online banking customers. Financial institutions spend millions of dollars to make sure that their electronic banking transactions are safe and secure. Banks use the latest Internet security technology, including secure communications, firewalls, encryption, and operating systems that have been designed to provide maximum security. They encrypt your personal data, including your password, when it is in transit to prevent third parties from accessing your information.

> **BLOOPER ALERT**
> Don't use the same password for online banking that you use for other insecure websites. Create a unique password just for your online banking.

LINGO

Encryption means the data is scrambled so it cannot be read by anyone who might infiltrate the transaction.

Sandy's tip

Your Social Security number is the key to your identity. Don't give it out online. Don't keep your Social Security card in your wallet. If you live in one of the few states that still use Social Security numbers on a driver's license, keep it as secure as possible.

Banks use many types of software, from simple to sophisticated. Some, such as Citibank, allow you to access online information with a password; some require that you download special encrypting software; some, such as Swiss banks, might use special software plus a one-time access code every time you log on.

You can generally determine if encryption is being used by checking to see if the padlock icon on your browser is locked. If the padlock icon is unlocked, encryption is not being used. See Chapter 3, "Shopping Online for Fun and Savings," for more information on secure websites.

Although banks are very responsible and have protection in place, you are responsible for keeping your banking information confidential. Don't share your password, account numbers, personal identification information, or other account data with anyone, including any other companies or services providers.

You are also responsible for notifying the bank about lost or stolen information or suspected fraudulent activity. In case you're wondering if you are protected from online fraud, the FDIC website at www.fdic.gov states: "Federal laws and rules may limit your liability for unauthorized transactions and set procedures for correcting errors. The Electronic Fund Transfer Act (EFTA) and the Federal Reserve Board's 'Regulation E' offer consumer protections, especially if you report a problem to your financial institution within specified time periods."

While we are talking about security, you will also want to make sure that your computer is fully protected. Install a good antivirus program and a firewall, and update them regularly. Also update your operating system and Internet browser software often. For more information on these and other security topics, pick up a copy of *Sandy Berger's Great Age Guide to the Internet*.

For more information on safety while banking online, check out the FDIC tips for Safe Internet Banking at www.fdic.gov/bank/individual/online/safe.html (see Figure 5.1).

Sandy's tip
Review your bank statement as soon as it arrives and report any suspicious or unauthorized transactions promptly.

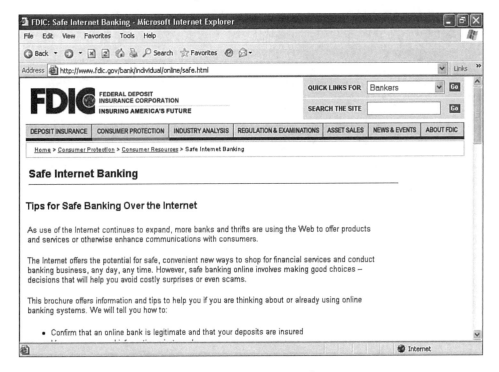

FIGURE 5.1
The FDIC Safe Internet Banking website has great information on safe online banking.

Other Financial Aids

Computers and the Internet are extremely helpful to all facets of financial living. You can use the Internet for all your financial news, learn more about finances, file your taxes, and even clean up your credit report more easily than ever before.

Information-Filled Financial Websites

There is so much to learn about finances. If you follow the financial news online, you might not have to subscribe to the *Wall Street Journal* anymore. There are many financial websites that give you all the news, plus interesting articles explaining what finance and economics are all about. Some also offer investing opportunities. Whether you are a seasoned financial expert or are just getting your feet wet in the financial world, there is sure to be a website for you.

Here are just a few to check out to get you started:

- **Bloomberg.com**–www.bloomberg.com/
- **CNN Money**–http://money.cnn.com/
- **MSN Money Central**–http://moneycentral.msn.com/home.asp
- **Reuters**–www.reuters.com
- **Yahoo! Finance**–http://finance.yahoo.com/

Other websites give you direct information on consumer protection issues, identity theft, online banking, and financial education. One of the best sites of this type is FirstGov, a government website that has a special section for consumers on money issues, as shown in Figure 5.2. You can find it at www.consumer.gov/yourmoney.htm.

File Your Taxes Online

In 2004, 61 million individual tax returns were filed electronically. The IRS has set up a free e-filing program and encourages e-filing. Why not? This is a big money saver for the IRS. But e-filing has benefits for the taxpayer as well. E-filing produces fewer errors by both IRS employees and taxpayers. You can file your taxes without leaving home. You will get your refund faster. And last but not least, in most states you can file your state taxes at the same time.

FIGURE 5.2
The FirstGov for Consumers website will give you information on everything money related.

Several tax-planning software programs are available that fill out the forms for you quickly and easily, making filing taxes easier than ever. The two most popular tax programs are H&R Block's TaxCut (www.hrblock.com) and Intuit's TurboTax (www.turbotax.com) program. The TurboTax program integrates well with Quicken because they are both from the same company. Microsoft and H&R Block work together, so the TaxCut program works very well with Microsoft Money.

Several other tax programs are available, including Intuit's ItsDeductible (www.itsdeductible.com), as shown in Figure 5.3. ItsDeductible uses IRS guidelines to determine the value of your donated items. It is geared at maximizing your tax savings for items that are usually undervalued or ignored.

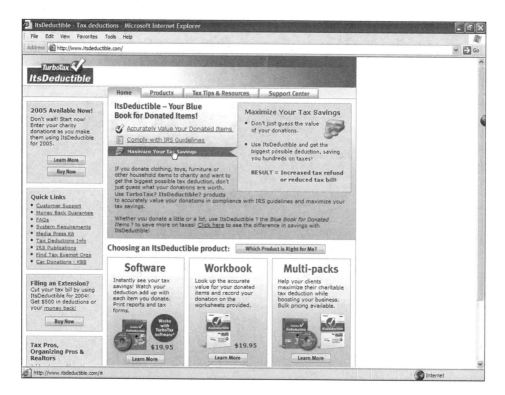

FIGURE 5.3
The Intuit ItsDeductible program gives you an accurate value for your donated items.

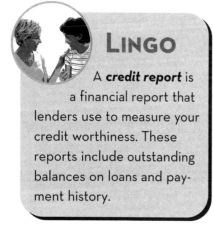

LINGO

A *credit report* is a financial report that lenders use to measure your credit worthiness. These reports include outstanding balances on loans and payment history.

Credit Reports

Identity theft is rampant in today's world. Financial experts recommend checking your credit reports on a regular basis to protect yourself against this evil. If someone else is using your identity, her financial transactions will appear on your credit report. Possible inaccuracies might be affecting your credit scores and preventing you from getting loans or costing you more on your credit card and insurance rates.

The three major credit agencies are

- **Equifax**—www.equifax.com/

- **Experian**—www.experian.com/

- **TransUnion**—www.transunion.com/

A recent amendment to the federal Fair Credit Reporting Act requires that each of the three nationwide consumer reporting companies provide you with a free copy of your credit report every 12 months. These reports are not sent automatically. You must request them. Equifax, Experian, and TransUnion have sponsored a website called AnnualCreditReport.com (at www.annualcreditreport.com) where you can apply for all three reports online. This website also gives you instructions for receiving these free reports by phone or mail. This new law makes it easy to monitor your credit reports on a regular basis.

LINGO

Identity theft is the title given to the act of stealing the identity of others by using their Social Security number, credit cards, and other stolen personal information. The thief can run up bills for the victims and are often able to open new accounts.

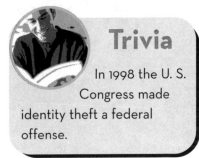

Trivia

In 1998 the U. S. Congress made identity theft a federal offense.

Retirement Planning

Planning for your retirement can be a difficult and time-consuming task, but Internet resources can lessen the load.

Many insurance companies have excellent information on their websites regarding retirement planning. For instance, the State Farm Insurance website has a great information website at www.statefarm.com/lifevents/retire.htm. MetLife has a questionnaire (http://198.65.242.50/metlife) that you can fill out to find out how long your retirement savings will last, as shown in Figure 5.4.

FIGURE 5.4
The Metlife website can help you determine how long your retirement savings will last.

You will also want to check out some of the major financial websites, such as the MSN Money Retirement and Wills area at http://moneycentral.msn.com/retire/home.asp. It has everything from How to Live Well in Retirement to Retirement Strategies for Late Starters.

Even websites that are not necessarily financial in nature have some good retirement planning tools. For instance, the About Retirement Planning area at http://retireplan.about.com has some great retirement articles, and the AARP Retirement Income area at www.aarp.org/money/financial_planning/retirement_income also has good information on the retirement account types.

To get down to the nitty-gritty, planning for retirement involves finding out what Social Security benefits you might have waiting for you. The Social Security Online website at www.ssa.gov/r&m1.htm calculates your benefits, enables you to learn about Social Security programs, and helps you decide when to retire (see Figure 5.5). You might want to visit the Internal Revenue Service Retirement Plans Community at www. irs.gov/retirement. This gives you information on how retirement plans are affected by taxes. It also has informational newsletters.

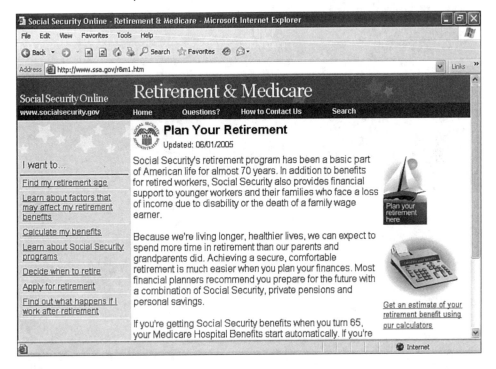

FIGURE 5.5
The Social Security Online Retirement & Medicare website will help you plan your retirement.

Finding Loans, Mortgages, and Insurance Online

By now there is no one who hasn't heard the ditech (www.ditech.com) commercials where this online loan service is taking mortgage loan business away from banks. LendingTree at www.lendingtree.com is another large online loan company. Lending Tree advertises that you can get up to four real loan offers in minutes. Although you might not want to actually secure your loan online, websites like this can be good for gathering information.

If you are in the market for a loan, you can also use free online loan calculators to determine how much different rates and amounts will affect your payment amounts. Check out the loan calculator at Bankrate.com at http://www.bankrate.com/brm/popcalc2.asp. You can see how easy it is to use in Figure 5.6.

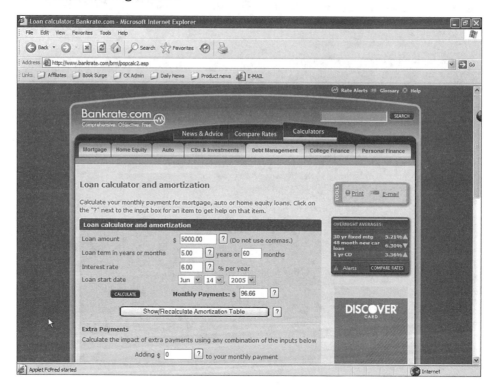

FIGURE 5.6
The Bankrate.com loan calculator gives you your payment amount in seconds.

You can also shop for insurance online. Every major insurance company has a website and some of them allow you to consult with an advisor online. All have a ton of information on their websites. Here are just a few of the major insurance websites:

- **Allstate Insurance**—www.allstate.com

- **Hartford Insurance**—www.thehartford.com

- **Geico Auto Insurance**—www.geico.com

- **Metropolitan Life Insurance Company**—www.metlife.com

- **Nationwide Mutual**—www.nationwide.com

- **State Farm Insurance**—www.statefarm.com

BLOOPER ALERT

Just like in your junk mail or TV ads, there are some insurance and loan websites that will take you for a ride. Check out the company, read the fine print, and check with consumer organizations before you agree to anything.

Investment Trading and Management on the Web

The Internet has opened the exclusive and often mysterious world of investing to the average computer user. Not only does the Internet offer information, research, and current data, but it also presents the investor with a whole new world of online trading. Internet and investing—millions are enjoying the benefits that these two big *i*'s offer when they are linked together.

To use the Internet to the fullest for your investment trading, you need to compare the services of stockbrokers, full-service brokerages, discount brokerages, and online trading houses.

In making a choice of which type of broker to use, determine the services you need. For advice and research, you need a full-service broker. If you want to do your own research and make your own decisions, try using a discount broker. Right now, there are many brokerage houses that specialize in online trading. The substantial discount that online brokers offer on their commission rates is a real attraction.

Online Trading Basics

Online trading has exploded in recent years as investors are becoming more self-confident and comfortable with their computers, the Internet, and their own investment skills. Online trading is a hot topic. A recent search on the Internet for "online trading" produced more than 20,000 results.

Online brokerage houses allow you to access account information at a moment's notice and place trades 24 hours a day, 7 days a week. With the growing number of online discount brokers, deciding which one to use can be an overwhelming endeavor. Although cost might be your first priority when choosing an online broker, you should also check out the website's ease of use, system responsiveness, and reliability. How difficult is it to actually make a trade? Can you easily see the results of your entries? Can you correct errors easily? How can you access account information if you cannot get online? Can you get a copy of your monthly statement if the website is down?

After you decide on an online broker, you need to set up your account. You can often initiate this online. However, you might also have to fill out forms that have to be mailed to the broker. You also need to send funds to the company to have money in your account for active trading. After the account is set up, you receive an account number and a password. Placing your trades is easy. My first online trade took less than 30 minutes to complete, including learning how to navigate the website. As a matter of fact, after I placed my first online trade, I felt two distinct emotions. I had an immense sense of accomplishment and also a feeling of amazement. I couldn't believe that I had purchased 500 shares of stock with a few quick clicks of a mouse.

Managing Your Portfolio Online

After you make your stock and bond purchases, you will probably want to follow some individual stocks on a regular basis. You might also want to keep your eye on targeted stocks for a possible future purchase. Internet users have many options for setting up a personal portfolio online. America Online has an excellent portfolio management tool. Many of the financial websites on the Internet offer their own personal portfolio program. Excite (www.excite.com), MyYahoo! (http://my.yahoo.com), and several other web search engine/portals offer a portfolio tracker free of charge to any Internet user. These sites also offer quotes, news items, and other pertinent investment information.

Although building an online portfolio is generally an easy task, deciding which website to use for your portfolio is not easy. You can use the website of the brokerage house you trade with to follow your portfolio, but you might want to try out others as well. There are many good sites available. Most are free of charge and are easy to use. One of the biggest differences between the sites is how much and what type of information they track and how it is displayed. Your best bet is to try several sites before you decide on the one you will use. Create a personal portfolio by entering just a few stocks. Then work with those stocks to see if you like the way the information is presented and formatted. Try out as many of the personal portfolio features as you can. Then do the same with the next website. If you spend just an hour or so a day, you will have checked out many of the popular sites within a week. After trying various sites, you will probably find one that you like. After your complete personal portfolio is set up, you can see at a glance how your stocks are performing at any time.

The type and costs of portfolio services offered by various online brokerages vary greatly. Most brokerages make stock quotes available online. When visiting the various online trading sites, make sure you notice if the quotes are real time quotes or not. Stock quotes given on some of the sites are delayed by up to 15 minutes.

Brokerage Websites

Ameritrade (www.ameritrade.com) markets its brokerage house as friendly, with superior customer service positioned on the cutting edge of technology. This company offers a large choice of trading options with low commissions. At Ameritrade, investors might place trades on the Internet, with the Touchtone System, or through a broker.

The Ameritrade website has several trading tools, as shown in Figure 5.7. These tools include trade triggers that set orders in advance to be sent automatically, streaming quotes, intra-day charts, and real-time account information.

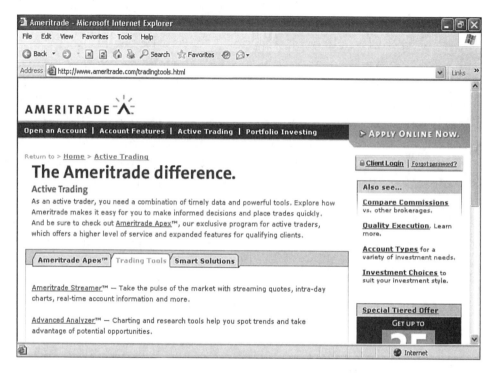

FIGURE 5.7
The Ameritrade website has a myriad of trading tools.

Charles Schwab, at www.schwab.com, is a well-known brokerage house. From its home page Schwab markets its breadth of products, online trading, extra services, and web reliability as well as its advice and planning services. A fun feature is the free equity ratings to help investors make better stock decisions. Charles Schwab invites its customers to manage their accounts, place trade orders, and get independent research all in one place.

E*Trade's home page at www.etrade.com is set up like file folders than can be opened to access your account, buy and sell stocks, and so forth. It is known for its low pricing for stock trades. In 2005, E*Trade won a Webby Award (The Web equivalent of an Oscar) as the best banking/bill-paying website of 2005. So, obviously, E*Trade has plenty of other services to go along with its brokerage service.

Merrill Lynch (www.ml.com) provides securities and brokerage trading, as well as other financial services.

At Morgan Stanley (www.morganstanley.com) you can check the status of your holdings, trade, buy or sell, get up-to-the-minute news releases, real-time stock quotes, and end-of-year tax summaries.

Several other online brokers are known for their inexpensive online trading. Look at Scottrade at www.scottrade.com and Harrisdirect at www.harrisdirect.com. Some of the websites listed previously also have excellent online trading prices. Pricing information changes too frequently to be listed here and a variety of restrictions can apply. At some sites you might get cheaper trades if you have a certain amount in an account with the company you are trading at. Check the websites for the most current price information and restrictions.

Researching Stocks and Bonds

The Internet is also a great place to research the companies that you might want to invest in. For general financial news, try CBS MarketWatch (www.cbs.marketwatch.com), as shown in Figure 5.8. For more specific information, be sure to visit the company's website. You might also want to check out some great investment sites such as the Motley Fool (www.fool.com) and the Raging Bull (www.ragingbull.com). Both of these sites allow you to keep an online portfolio, get stock quotes and financial news, and participate in chat rooms and other online activities. I like the design of the Motley Fool better, but both have excellent content. Even Yahoo! has a finance area that can be found at http://finance.yahoo.com. This website is a comprehensive research, bill-paying, banking, loan, and insurance website filled with great information.

After you have used the Internet as a tool for investing, you will never want to go back to your old ways again. The web offers the average investor more options to manage his money than ever before.

FIGURE 5.8
There is always plenty of financial news at the CBS MarketWatch website.

Sandy's Summary

Computers and the Internet have sent large waves through financial waters. With these tools, anyone can completely automate her finances. Financial programs such as Microsoft Money and Intuit's Quicken balance your checkbook, schedule payments, track your spending, and help you budget your money. Online banking eliminates long waits in teller lines and enables you to do your banking anytime, day or night, right from your own home. You can transfer funds, pay bills, and track purchases online.

Millions of people now use online banking and banks are providing safe and secure electronic banking for all. You should, however, be careful with your password, protect your own computer with an antivirus program and firewall, and check your bank statements regularly, reporting any discrepancies quickly. You should also protect yourself from identity theft by checking your credit reports regularly. This is easy with online resources.

The Internet is filled with financial websites that give you the current financial news and help you learn about economics and finance. If you are into the stock market, there are also many places to trade online and get stock quotes and other investment information. Don't discount the Internet as the place to find loans, mortgages, and insurance. You can even file your taxes online.

With all this ease-of-use, you can't go wrong computerizing your finances to make your life a little easier.

Sandy Berger

Chapter 6

Digital Photography and Instant Printing

"Any sufficiently advanced technology is indistinguishable from magic."
—Arthur C. Clarke

When I saw my first instant camera back in the fifties, I was totally amazed. I could barely imagine a camera that allowed you to snap a picture and get instant results. That old Polaroid camera is probably sitting in a museum somewhere. As ground-breaking as it was, the technological developments that followed were even more mind-boggling.

Digital cameras, together with computers, printers, and scanners, have revolutionized the world of photography. Today we not only have instant results, we have completely done away with film and are still able to produce spectacular photographs. Digital photography allows even amateur photographers to look like professionals. We have come a long way from the streaky photographs of that old Polaroid.

Instead of film, digital cameras use a memory card to hold the photos. You never have to worry about the cost of film because the memory card can be used over and over again. Because you can see the picture right after you press the shutter, you can delete and retake any photo that you did not get just right. The photos can be transferred directly from the camera to a computer for editing, printing, and archiving.

Sandy's tip
Buy your digital camera from a reputable source who is willing to help you with any problems you might have.

LINGO

Memory cards are small, removable modules that are used to store information. They are sometimes referred to as flash cards or media cards. Several types are currently available, including CompactFlash, SmartMedia, Memory Stick, and xD-Picture Card.

What Makes a Camera Digital?

A digital camera is a filmless camera that performs many of the same functions as a 35 millimeter camera, but it offers much more versatility. Although some digital cameras look like traditional cameras, they are fundamentally different.

Digital photography is unique in the way it captures and stores an image. Instead of film, digital imaging technology uses a grid of many very small sensors that translate what enters the lens into data. This data is transferred to an image file that is then recorded on the camera's own internal memory or on a reusable memory card. After a photo is in the camera's memory, it is ready for printing, viewing, or uploading to a computer.

Digital cameras have come a long way since their introduction a few years ago. You can buy them in many shapes and sizes (see Figure 6.1). The four basic categories of digital cameras are

- *Professional* cameras are for serious photographers. They allow you to manually adjust all the settings, including white balance, aperture settings, shutter speeds, and so on. These include, but are not limited to, Single Lens Reflex (SLR) cameras with interchangeable lenses.

- *Prosumer* cameras are for the part-time professional or the amateur who wants to try his hand at a high-end camera. They are meant for the consumer who wants the camera to auto-adjust and choose the settings for him but also might want to adjust the settings manually.

- *Point-and-shoot* cameras handle all the settings for you. They allow you to take a quick shot without detailed photographic knowledge. Many are small enough to fit in a pocket or purse.

- *Mini-cameras* are those that are so small they can be built into cell phones or hang off a key chain. Although many of these are being created just for novelty, they are becoming more and more useful as the quality improves.

As the numbers and types of digital cameras increase, the lines between these various types of cameras begin to blur. But the trick to purchasing a digital camera is to always match up your photographic capabilities and expectations to the capabilities and features of the camera itself.

Trivia

Kodak was not the name of a person. Rather, it was the name of the Eastman Kodak Company's first camera. After the picture was snapped on the Kodak camera, the film was sent to the Eastman Dry Plate and Film Co. in Rochester, NY for developing.

FIGURE 6.1

Digital cameras come in many shapes and sizes.

Understanding Digital Photography

Digital cameras are newfangled pieces of equipment. Even if you were very familiar with film cameras, you will find that digital photography uses new terminology as well as different ways to capture and display the image. A digital camera records color images as intensities of red, green, and blue. The images are captured by an image sensor chip in the camera. They are then stored on the camera's on-board storage, or more often on a removable memory card. The quality of the photo depends on the quality of the image sensor chip and the amount of detail that it records. This is called resolution, and you will see it measured in megapixels.

With film cameras you had to determine the type of film that was best for the photos you wanted to capture. When working with digital cameras you don't have to worry about the film because there is none! Instead you have to understand the different file formats that your camera uses to save the images. You also have to be concerned with the type of batteries your camera uses and battery life. Don't worry, though. It is easy to learn the basics of digital photography, and the reward of instant pictures is worth any time you invest in the learning process.

Resolution and Image Quality

Resolution refers to the sharpness and clarity of an image. A digital camera measures resolution in pixels. The higher the number of pixels, the higher the resolution. The higher the resolution, the better the quality, sharpness, and clarity of an image.

Camera resolution is measured in megapixels, with each megapixel equal to one million pixels. You see cameras that have one, two, three, or more megapixels.

LINGO

The resolution of a camera is measured in **megapixels**. Each megapixel contains one million pixels. A **pixel** is a single point in a graphic image.

Basically, the number of megapixels you need in a camera depends on how you want to use the photos. Putting pictures on a website or emailing photos that will only be viewed on the computer screen doesn't require a high resolution. In fact, for these tasks, a camera resolution of one megapixel or less is adequate. Photos taken at lower resolution create smaller files, so using low resolutions for the Web and email also keeps the file size small and makes downloads speedy.

LINGO

To **crop** is to cut off the sides of a picture to make it the proper size, to remove superfluous areas, or to focus on a certain area.

A 1-megapixel camera might be good for posting photos on the Web, but it will not produce quality printouts. As you increase the number of megapixels in the camera, you increase the quality of the printed photos, and the size at which those photos will look good. So if you plan to print pictures, choose a camera with a higher resolution. For the average user, a 3-megapixel photograph rivals prints from a 35mm camera.

Remember that the higher the number of pixels, the higher the resolution; the higher the resolution, the larger you can print a photo with good results. A camera with 7- or 8-megapixels produces very high-quality photos.

A photo taken with a higher megapixel camera also has other advantages, as well. If you want to use just a portion of the photo, you can crop the photo and still retain the details and the quality. For example, you take a great group family photo. After looking at the picture, you notice that Aunt Edna has never taken such a nice photo. You would love to have a picture that only shows her face. With a simple photo-editing program you can easily crop the photo to show only Aunt Edna's face. If the photo was taken with a 1-megapixel camera, Aunt Edna is sure to look grainy and blurry when you print the cropped photo. However, if you used a 6- or 7-megapixel camera, she will probably look just as great as she did in the group photo. Many digital cameras have scene settings. These preprogrammed settings allow you to choose the type of photo you are taking and then the camera adjusts the white balance and other settings. You can often choose from different scenes such as portrait, landscape, night scene, and fireworks. These are a boon to the novice photographer.

File Storage

Most digital cameras use a removable, rewritable memory card for storing photographs after they are taken. CompactFlash and SmartMedia are two of the most popular types of removable media. Both are very small disks—less than one quarter the size of a floppy disk. There are also several other types of memory cards including the Sony Memory Stick, Secure Digital Cards, xD-Picture Cards, IBM Microdrives, and MultiMediaCards (see Figure 6.2). Each of these is a slightly different shape and size, so they are not interchangeable. If you already own a piece of equipment that uses one type of card, you might want to purchase a camera that uses the same type of card so you can share the storage cards between your devices. Each card is available in different capacities. Some hold only 16MB of information. Some hold 256MB. Some are even larger. A card that holds 16MB will look exactly the same as the card that holds 256MB. The label on the card is the only external indication of how much data the card holds.

The number of photos that will fit on a memory card depend not only on the capacity of the memory card, but also on the megapixels of the camera and the quality settings. Pictures taken with the camera set on the highest quality setting take up more room on the memory card than those taken at a lower quality setting. Higher megapixel cameras also need more room to store their photos. For example, given similar quality settings, my 2-megapixel camera can fit more than 100 pictures on its 128MB media card. My 5-megapixel camera can hold only about 50 photos on the same size card. In general, a 128MB card is adequate for most folks, but if you

Sandy's tip

Stay away from any camera that only stores photos in the camera itself. Purchasing a camera that stores photos on a memory card allows you to add more storage space by simply purchasing a larger memory card.

expect to take a lot of photos and your camera has a high pixel count, you might want to consider a 256MB or larger card.

Memory Stick

Compact Flash

SmartMedia

XD-Picture

FIGURE 6.2
There are many types of memory cards.

Sandy's tip
If your camera uses regular AA or AAA batteries, check your user manual before you use rechargeable batteries. Some manufacturers recommend only non-rechargeable batteries.

Batteries

Batteries and battery life are of prime importance with digital cameras. Traditional cameras don't need a lot of power so their batteries can last for months. If you don't use your flash attachment often, they could last for years. Digital cameras are very different. They need a lot of juice to power their viewing screens and other mechanical parts. Be sure to look for a camera that gives you long battery life.

Be aware that different digital cameras use different types of batteries. Some use special rechargeable battery packs that can only be purchased from the camera manufacturer, and can only be used in certain cameras from that manufacturer. Some use regular AA or AAA batteries.

Each battery type has specific advantages and disadvantages. If your camera uses a rechargeable battery, there is no extra cost for batteries. You simply put the battery pack into the charger that came with the camera and plug it into a wall outlet to recharge. The drawback is that it can take a long time for the battery to recharge and if your battery runs low, you cannot take pictures until you recharge the battery. With a camera that uses regular AA or AAA batteries, you can carry a spare set of batteries or replenish your batteries with a stop at just about any grocery, drug, or convenience store, but you will pay more for your battery power.

Because downloading photos to the computer poses a considerable drain on the batteries, it might be smart to consider purchasing an AC adapter to use for downloading or when you are near an electrical receptor. You might also want to consider using a card reader that does not use any of your battery power to transfer your photographs to the computer. We'll talk about card readers and other transfer devices later in this chapter in the "Adding Smart Accessories" section.

BLOOPER ALERT

Most digital cameras display an icon when the battery power is getting low. When you see your battery power warning, recharge or replace the batteries immediately. Taking pictures with very low power can corrupt the files on the memory card.

File Formats

If you are already using a certain type of software to manage your photos, make sure that your digital camera produces photos in the file format your software can accept. The most common format in use today is called JPEG. It is possible to use your image-editing software to convert photos from one format to another, but you can save yourself that extra step by checking for compatibility before you purchase your camera.

LINGO

JPEG (Joint Photographic Experts Group). Pronounced "jay-peg." It is a standard still-image format that has become very popular due to its excellent compression capabilities. JPEGs, often referred to as jpg files, are widely used for photographic images.

Several other file formats are RAW and TIFF. These files produce more detail than JPEGs, but they create much larger files. Generally, these two file formats are used when you want to perform very detailed editing on the photos.

Ease of Connection

Many older cameras hooked up to the computer through a serial port. This was a slow type of connection that often required rebooting the computer when attaching the camera. Most newer cameras hook up to the computer through a USB connection. USB ports are found on most computers with Windows 98 or later and all Mac computers.

A USB connection transfers your photos quickly. It is easy to set up and is hot-swappable. *Hot-swappable* means that after you attach the camera, the computer recognizes the camera without the need to reboot. Computers with Windows 98 might need to have a special driver installed to tell the computer to recognize the connection, while later operating systems won't even need that step. Just hook up the camera to your USB port and you are able to transfer the photos to your computer.

LINGO

FireWire is a very fast bus (type of connection) often used for transferring audio and video files. FireWire was originally developed by Apple but is compatible with PCs that are equipped with a FireWire port.

Some of the newer cameras, especially video cameras, hook up to the computer via a FireWire connection. FireWire, also called IEEE 1394, is faster than USB and is especially useful when dealing with videos, which are usually very large files. All Apple computers have FireWire ports, but not many PCs come with a FireWire port as a standard feature. You can order a FireWire port when you purchase a new PC. Depending on the configuration and age of your computer you can often add this type of connection by adding a FireWire card if your computer does not have one installed.

Optical and Digital Zoom

As most of you already know, zoom is a function of a camera that makes images seem closer up. In traditional cameras there is only one type of zoom. In digital cameras, there are two: optical zoom and digital zoom.

Optical zoom is the type of zoom that is found in standard cameras. Elements in the lens move to create a magnified field of view. This makes the object appear closer. When using optical zoom, the image clarity is the same as the clarity normally produced by the camera.

sandy's tip

A good zoom always comes in handy. It is worth spending a few dollars more to get a camera with a good optical zoom.

Digital zoom is a kind of simulated zoom that is created digitally. The camera takes a small portion of the image and through a mathematical calculation, resizes the image to a larger size. Because digital zoom reduces the resolution of the image, it produces results that are not as clear as optical zoom. Digital zoom, which requires no moving parts, is much cheaper to add to a camera, so you will see it in many low-end cameras. Digital zoom produces results that are obviously inferior to optical zoom. Most photos taken with only a digital zoom will be grainy when printed any larger than 4" × 6".

Many of today's cameras have both optical and digital zoom. The digital zoom more or less supplements the optical zoom. If you like using a zoom lens, get a camera with adequate optical zoom for the best clarity so the digital zoom doesn't have to kick in, even if it is available.

The digital and optical zoom I have been talking about is built into the camera. These types of zoom are available on most point-and-shoot digital cameras. If you are a serious photographer, you can purchase a Single Lens Reflex (SLR) camera that allows you to change lenses. With an SLR camera you can buy many types of zoom lenses.

LCD Camera Screens

Most digital cameras have LCD screens, as shown in Figure 6.3. They are used to see exactly how the picture that was just taken turned out. Click the shutter and, presto, you look at the camera's screen and see the photo you just took. In many cameras (SLR cameras are the exception) the LCD screen can also be used to view the picture you are about to take. Some cameras have a viewfinder plus an LCD screen and you can use either to set up the picture. Be sure you are comfortable with the viewing method used by a digital camera before you make your purchase. Also check out the size and clarity of the screen. If you can, try the camera in sunlight to see if the LCD is viewable in bright light.

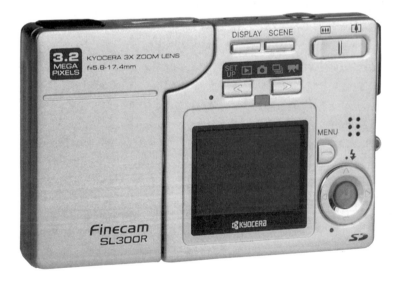

FIGURE 6.3
Digital cameras have very useful LCD screens.

These LCD screens are very useful and provide one of the best features of all. If you take a bad photo, just press the Erase or Delete button to dump the dud and retake the picture until you get it right.

Things to Consider Before You Buy

Like film-based cameras, the more you pay equates to higher quality and more features when purchasing a camera. The following sections cover the things that you should consider when purchasing a digital camera.

Ease of Use

Any camera you buy should be easy to use. Look for large, easy-to-understand buttons and straightforward documentation. Who wants to go through a time-consuming learning curve if you don't have to? Remember, the more features your camera has, the more complex it will be to operate. Try to match the camera's complexity to your photography experience. If you understand color balance and aperture priorities, you might want to go for a full-featured camera. If not, look for a point-and-shoot variety that offers you good results without a lot of manipulation.

BLOOPER ALERT

What you see is not always what you get. Most computer display screens have very low resolutions. That means jagged lines on screen might smooth out when they print. Also the color you see on the screen might not match what is printed.

Check out the Software

Almost all digital cameras come with software that allows you to download the photos from your camera to your computer. Often that software also enables you to edit the photos and make simple corrections. You should base your camera decision on the camera itself. Look at the software that comes with your camera as an added bonus. If it performs well, you will be a bit happier. If the software that accompanies the camera does not perform to your expectations, you can always purchase additional software, such as Microsoft's Picture It for the PC or Adobe's Photoshop Elements, which is available for both PC and Mac.

Trivia

You probably know that Thomas Edison invented the light bulb, but did you know that in 1889 he also invented the first commercially successful camera?

Mac or PC

The photos from most digital cameras can be transferred to either a PC or a Mac. Memory or media card readers can be easily attached to either PC or Mac to quickly transfer the photos to the computer. There is, however, a big difference in the software used for transferring. Almost all digital cameras will come with software for the PC. Often a digital camera will come with software for both PC and Mac. If you are using a Mac and you want to take advantage of the included software, make sure that there is a Mac version of the software available. If you have OS X, you also have iPhoto, which will enable you to download photos from your camera to your Mac.

Adding Smart Accessories

When you purchase a digital camera, you might want to consider getting a few accessories to go along with your puchase. Of course you can add a camera case, and with some cameras you can also add different lenses and flash attachments, but these are not the accessories I am talking about here. I want you to consider some of the small purchases that will make using your digital camera easier to use, such as memory card readers, larger memory cards, and extra rechargeable battery packs.

Memory Card Readers

Using a card reader is the easiest way to transfer digital photos from your camera to your computer. You don't need to bother with drivers and software programs; you just need an inexpensive memory (media) card reader. You can purchase a reader that accepts one type of memory card or you can purchase a reader that accommodates several types of cards. If you have several devices that use different cards, the latter can be useful. So if your PDA takes a SmartMedia card and your camera takes a CompactFlash card, you can use a multislotted card reader to transfer the pictures from the CompactFlash to the SmartMedia. Then you will be able to show your pictures on your PDA.

When you hook the card reader up to the computer with the attached USB cable, the device appears as a removable drive. On a PC, you can find the drive by double-clicking the My Computer icon on your desktop. Then you can drag and drop or copy the pictures to your hard drive. Mac users can also use the same card readers to attach to their USB ports. The photos appear right on the desktop. It's as easy as pie and you don't wear down your camera's batteries during the transfer process.

> ### Sandy's tip
> Some computers now come with slots to accommodate different types of memory cards. If you are lucky enough to have a computer with this type of slot, you won't have to purchase a memory card reader.

Extra Batteries

If your digital camera uses manufacturer-specific rechargeable batteries, purchasing an extra battery pack might be a good idea. Then you can recharge one while you use the other. Or, if you will be taking a lot of photos, you can charge them both up to make sure you have the power you need to create all those digital memories.

Although AA and AAA batteries are widely available, it is always wise to carry enough to replenish your camera when needed. Remember that when it comes to technology or digital equipment, Murphy's Law of "whatever can go wrong will" always applies.

Larger Memory Cards

Most cameras come with small memory cards of 16MB or 32MB just to get you started. After the memory card fills up, you will not be able to take anymore pictures unless you delete some of the pictures on the card or move the pictures to a computer or other device. You don't want to have your camera say Card Full just when you are ready to take that shot of the winning soccer goal.

Sandy's tip

Many cameras have four quality settings: quality, high, medium, and low. The higher quality settings give you more clarity, but also produce larger files.

A larger memory card should be one of your first accessory purchases. Prices on memory cards have plummeted. That means you can probably afford a much larger card than the one that came with your camera. The number of photos that will fit on a memory card depend not only on the capacity of the memory card, but also on the megapixels of the camera and the quality settings. Photos taken at higher pixel levels produce larger files that take up more room. So if you have an 8-megapixel camera, you will need a larger memory card than you will need for a 2-megapixel camera.

For a quick comparison, take this example. If you have a 64MB memory card and your 5-megapixel camera is set to the highest quality settings, you will be able to take approximately 24 pictures. With the same highest quality settings, a 2-megapixel camera will be able to fit about 61 photos on the same 64MB card.

Quality of the Company

For a quality digital camera, look at the company behind the camera as much as the camera itself. Luckily, with digital cameras, finding a quality company is fairly easy. Many traditional camera makers have made the move to digital. Some of the top vendors in the digital camera market are Sony, Canon, Kodak, Olympus, Nikon, and Minolta. Many of these vendors have been making cameras since the early 1900s. Others in the digital market include Fuji, HP, Epson, and Casio. If you know these companies and have been happy with their cameras in the past, you will want to check them out when you make your digital camera purchase. Make sure that the company provides adequate support for the product. A good way to check out the support options, as well as the available cameras, is to visit the camera

Trivia

Eastman Kodak's Brownie camera cost $1.00 when it was introduced in 1900.

manufacturer's website. Remember that these websites are sure to be a bit biased, but they have great information. Here are a few:

- **Canon**—www.canon.com

- **Casio**—www.casio.com

- **Epson**—www.epson.com

- **Fuji**—www.fujifilm.com

- **HP**—www.hp.com

- **Kodak**—www.kodak.com

- **Minolta**—http://konicaminolta.com

- **Nikon**—www.nikon.com

- **Olympus**—www.olympus.com

- **Sony**—www.sony.com

Warranty

Know what is covered under the warranty. Check where the service providers are located. Are they local or will you have to send the camera in for service? In addition, check to see how easy it is to get repairs done after your warranty has expired.

Know Your Cameras Capabilities

Take the time to learn all about your new camera and how it works. The time you invest in reading the manual and taking practice shots will reap endless benefits. Also investigate the capabilities of your new camera thoroughly. Many digital cameras come with an S-Video connector that allows you to connect your camera to a television set for viewing and even creating a slideshow of your photographs.

Sandy's tip

You might not have needed the directions when you put the kid's wagon together, but it's different with digital photography. The best way to learn about your camera is to read the manual.

After you have acquired a digital camera, you will be overwhelmed with the fun and photographic potential the camera gives you when paired with your computer. Your energy and imagination will be challenged well. Impressive and valuable shots are now within your shutter sights.

Advice from Experts

You can certainly learn about digital cameras from friends and neighbors, but don't forget that with the Internet, expert advice is always at your fingertips. Of course you can search for information using a search engine, but you might also want to check out the websites of some of the big computer, camera, and printer manufacturers.

For instance, visit the Olympus website at www.olympusamerica.com and click on Digital Photography. Choose Digital Cameras and then click on the Learn tab. This area is filled with great free information. It has a series of excellent photography lessons and advice for buying as well as digital photography tips and tricks. At the Fujifilm Picture Your Life Creativity Center, at http://pictures.fujifilm.com, you will find more tips and even an area where you can get your questions answered by an expert. You will have to sign up for this service, but it is free. If you don't mind paying for photographic instruction, check out the Nikon School website at www.nikonschool.com. Although there is a cost, you can learn photography online from the comfort of your home.

Even Microsoft, which doesn't manufacturer cameras, offers tips for digital photography. At the Windows XP Digital Photography website, at www.microsoft.com/windowsxp/using/digitalphotography/learnmore/editing.mspx, Microsoft offers advice about fixing problems that occur in photos. It even tells you how to avoid taking photos that are beyond help, and gives a list of the more popular software programs with links to more information on each of those programs.

Editing and Organizing Digital Photos

After learning to use your digital camera, you will want to investigate how to improve photos, create collages, and develop other masterpieces. I'm not kidding. With some simple software, you can get stunning results.

The popularity of digital photography has given rise to a plethora of photo-editing and organizing software. Almost all of these tools allow you to repair and edit your photographs so that you can look and feel like a professional photographer. You can easily remove red eye and correct color or lighting problems in a photograph. You can also crop your photos so you print only the part you want, rotate pictures so they print right side up, and remove other minor flaws (or even a whole person!).

Photo-Editing Software

Before you go out and purchase any editing program, check out the software that came with your digital camera. The amount and quality of the software will vary, but almost all cameras include at least some basic software. Today many cameras include some wonderful software, but there are also a few unintuitive duds.

You might find that the software you already own is perfect for you. If, however, you want more powerful or better software, there are plenty of programs to choose from.

Adobe Photoshop Elements

The most famous photo-editing program is Adobe's Photoshop. At about $600, it is a heavy-duty program that will let you not only correct your photos, but also produce stunning creative photos. Learning Photoshop is almost a full-time job. If you are not ready for that kind of expense or time investment, you might want to look at the Adobe Photoshop Elements program. Elements is available for both PC and Mac. At less than $100, this program, like its big brother, is an excellent photo-editing program. With Photoshop Elements you can also get stunning results with less of a time investment. Photoshop Elements also does double-duty as a photo organization program (see Figure 6.4).

FIGURE 6.4
Photoshop Elements is a full-featured image editing program.

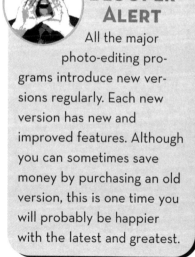

BLOOPER ALERT

All the major photo-editing programs introduce new versions regularly. Each new version has new and improved features. Although you can sometimes save money by purchasing an old version, this is one time you will probably be happier with the latest and greatest.

Photoshop Elements also boasts some of the more advanced features of the full version of Photoshop that have been modified to work with a single click of the mouse. You can add special effects and filters to give your photos a more creative look. You can change your photo to look like a charcoal sketch or even a watercolor painting.

After you start taking digital photographs, a program to help you organize and archive them is essential. You don't want photos to languish on your hard drive the way they used to accumulate in boxes in the closet. So get a program like Photoshop Elements to help.

Paint Shop Pro

Jasc Paint Shop Pro is another program that has high-end photo-editing capabilities at a reasonable price (see Figure 6.5) . At less than $100 this program is easy, yet it has plenty of robust editing tools. A beginner will feel more comfortable with this program. This is a PC-only program. Unfortunately, no Mac version is available.

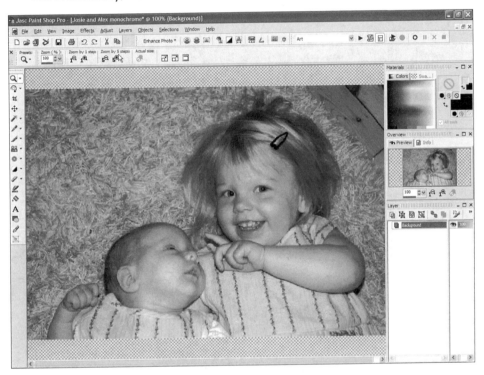

FIGURE 6.5
With Paint Shop Pro you can fix color problems, remove red eye, and resize and reposition photos, as well as accomplish many other editing tasks.

Nero PhotoShow Elite

Another excellent, less expensive, but capable program of this type is Nero PhotoShow Elite. It fits very well on the simple side of the scale. It includes uncomplicated tools that will help you edit and organize your photographs as well as create spectacular slideshows you can share with others. As with Photoshop Elements, Nero makes it easy to rotate, crop, auto-fix, and correct red eye. You can also add effects such as swirl, blur, and emboss. A variety of frames and captions are also provided for your added enjoyment. Again, this is a PC-only program with no Mac version available.

iPhoto

Mac users need not despair. iPhoto, shown in Figure 6.6, is a part of the Apple iLife software. It is a quality photo-editing software program. iPhoto has an excellent graphical interface and allows you to edit, organize, and share your photos with ease. Of course, you can modify brightness, straighten photos, and perform all the usual photo-editing tasks. With iPhoto you can even make picture albums and slideshows.

FIGURE 6.6
iPhoto is a very capable photo-editing program.

If you have the full iLife suite, you can take the images you edit in iPhoto and use them in other projects with applications such as iDVD and iMovie.

Other Photo-Editing Solutions

Look around and you will find many other photo programs to consider. A few of them are

- **Microsoft Picture It! (PC only)**—www.microsoft.com/products/imaging

- **Ulead PhotoImpact (PC and Mac)**—www.ulead.com

- **Picasa (PC only)**—www.picasa.com

- **HP Image Zone Express (PC only)**—www.hp.com/united-states/ize/home.html

For PC users, Picasa and HP Image Zone Express are good places to start. Both are free programs that have all the essential photo editing, organizing, and sharing tools. The HP Image Zone Express website also has tutorials.

To determine which photo program is for you, read about the programs at the manufacturers' websites and talk to friends about which programs they use and like. A few other things to look at are

- Get a program geared to your level of expertise. If you are a beginner, start with the easiest program and be ready to upgrade to a more complex program as your skills improve.

- Even if you are an expert, templates and wizards can be helpful. A wizard is a guide that will step you through the editing or creation process. A template is a prebuilt form that helps you create projects.

- Unless you have plenty of time to focus on learning programs, you will want to find one that is simple.

- Look at the program features and see which suit your interests. Many of these programs enable you to email your photos to friends and create slideshows, collages, greeting cards, and other projects.

Printers and Printing Options

A recent report from Lyra Research states that most digital camera photos are now printed at home using inkjet printers. It's not hard to figure out why. Printing pictures at home means we get instant results and also get to express our creativity.

Any printer can be used to print photos. Thermal dye printers produce the best quality, but because of their high cost, most home users will print their pictures on the more affordable inkjet printers. The explosion in digital photography has also caused a proliferation of new inkjet printers. Some inkjet printers are now made especially for printing photos.

Photo Printers

Some inkjet printers are labeled as photo printers. These types of printers usually have special ink cartridges and a higher print quality than your typical desktop printer (see Figure 6.7). Many photo printers can also print borderless photos with no white border on the outside. This is a special feature that is not usually included in regular inkjet printers.

Sandy's tip

Photo printers that have special color ink cartridges can produce better colors for your photos. So a photo printer that has eight color cartridges prints colors that are more realistic than a printer with only three color cartridges. Some photo printers even have different black cartridges to produce more realistic photographs.

Some of the newer photo printers also have a small LCD screen and slots for memory cards. You simply remove the memory card from your camera, insert it into the printer, view the photos on the LCD screen, and print the photos of your choice. This allows you to print directly from the memory card without having to use a computer. If you purchase a photo printer with these advanced features, make sure that the printer accepts the type of memory card used in your camera.

FIGURE 6.7
Photo printers enable you to print the images you want, right on the spot.

Paper Makes a Big Difference

The quality of a home-printed photograph is directly related to the quality of the paper that is used. Unfortunately, choosing the best photo paper can be very confusing due to labeling inconsistencies by manufacturers. Some paper will simply say Premium Glossy Photo Paper or Heavyweight Matte Photo Paper. Other paper is rated by weight, such as 46 lbs. Others will give brightness and sheen ratings, such as 93%. So try to purchase your paper from a reputable dealer who displays samples of the paper and/or will let you open the package to inspect the weight and quality.

It is best to start with a photo paper that is offered by the manufacturer of your printer. For instance, if you have an Epson printer, use

Epson photo paper. Although most printer manufacturers purchase their paper from another company, the printer manufacturer has calibrated its printer profiles and ink sets to perform best with its own branded paper. This usually gives better colors, contrast, and overall quality. If the manufacturer of your printer does not produce paper under its own brand, check with the company to see which brand of paper it recommends.

After you have seen the output using your manufacturer's paper, you can try other papers. You might have to adjust your photos by making them lighter or darker or adjusting contrast in your photo-editing software. Be ready to spend some money on different types of paper and to spend some time to trying out various combinations. After you find the paper that gives you the results you like, you can stick with that brand and those settings.

Specialty Papers

Don't limit yourself when it comes to printing on special paper. Investigate all your options. With the proper paper you can turn your photos into scrapbooks, calendars, or greeting cards. There is even paper available for creating photo stickers that children and grandchildren are sure to love.

When looking for specialized paper, check out the paper made by your printer's manufacturer first, but don't overlook third-party manufacturers. Some vendors, such as Burlington and Pictorico, concentrate on specialty paper. Burlington papers, available at various retail outlets as well as at www.burlingtonpaper.com, come in many varieties, including watercolor paper. With these special papers, you can simply add some special effects to your photograph with your photo-editing software and produce prints that look as good as paintings. Burlington also has holographic labels and holographic mailing seals. At Pictorico (www.pictorico.com) you can find Premium Canvas paper and Poly Silk Fabric paper. Both were created to make your photos look like real works of art. Pictorico also has full sheets of adhesive film you can use for creating bumper stickers and signs. Specialty paper can also be found for making magnets and mouse pads. Add a little imagination and the possibilities are endless.

Dealing with Ink

Inkjet printers are wonderful for printing photographs, creating colorful greeting cards, and printing web pages. They have routinely become less expensive while resolution, print speed, and print quality have increased. Even the technology behind the printers and ink has improved, making output look better and last longer. There is only one drawback to inkjet printers: ink can be costly.

I recently saw an inkjet printer that was available for $39. When I looked at print cartridges, I found that each cartridge cost $30. Purchasing ink for an inkjet printer can be problematic. You have several choices: purchase the more costly ink cartridges from the manufacturer, purchase remanufactured ink cartridges, or purchase refill kits to refill cartridges yourself.

When printing photographs, it is best to use the ink that is provided by your printer manufacturer. If, however, you really want to save some money by using third-party ink cartridges, you can print some photos and see if the quality is acceptable.

Be aware that most manufacturers frown on using anything other than their own cartridges. Of course, since print cartridges mean a lot of revenue to them, you would expect them to say this. Most printer manufacturers say that using refill kits or refurbished cartridges can damage print heads, start ink leaks, and produce inferior output. In many cases using third-party ink cartridges voids the printer warranty. Some lawyers say the manufacturers are simply using scare tactics because

Sandy's tip

If you are going on an extended vacation or won't be using your printer for more than a month, remove the print cartridges and carefully store them in an airtight container. This prevents the ink from drying up and clogging the print head.

Sandy's tip
Like traditional photographs, digital prints fade over time. The printer, paper, and ink you are using all affect the longevity. Check the documentation that came with your printer and/or the printer manufacturer's website for details. Storing photos under glass will extend their longevity.

invalidating the warranty for using other brand consumables would violate antitrust laws and the Magnuson-Moss Warranty Improvement Act. But manufacturers counter that the warranty is still intact; it simply will not cover damage caused by third-party ink and refilled cartridges. I suppose it will take some large class-action suit to settle that one. In the meantime, don't count on using your printer warranty without a battle if you use third-party sources for your ink.

Printer Settings

Printer settings are an important part of printing photographs. You must choose the proper paper settings in the printer setup. This is usually done by choosing Properties or Preferences from the Print menu and changing the settings under the Paper Setup or Paper Type, as shown in Figure 6.8. Depending on your printer, the choices might say something like glossy photo paper, coated paper, or premium photo paper. Sometimes the paper choices for some printers can also be chosen right on the printer itself. The printer lays down differing amounts of ink depending on the type of paper chosen. So if you choose plain paper in the settings but try to print on glossy paper or vice-versa, you are sure to be disappointed in the results.

After you have chosen the type of paper in the print settings, you should also look for other settings. Often you can choose from various quality modes, such as economy, normal, or photo quality. Depending on your printer, other options might also be available. See the manual that came with your printer to determine exactly what print settings you have available and how to access those settings.

FIGURE 6.8
You need to choose the type of paper in the printer settings.

Creative Printing Programs

Creative printing software helps you print photos and create printed projects. Many other programs, such as Paint Shop Pro and Photoshop Elements (discussed previously in this chapter), focus more on helping you create artistic graphics and adjust and edit photographs.

Software to help you print photos and to create projects such as calendars, greeting cards, and paper hats have been around for a long time.

The Print Shop by Broderbund (www.broderbund.com) was one of the first printer software programs I used. The first version was introduced in 1984. Over the years more than 20 versions have been created, each one better than the last. The Print Shop Deluxe helps you create a large variety of printed products. It has 16,000 project templates and more than 310,000 images to help you with your printing projects. Although The Print Shop can help you make calendars, another Broderbund program called Calendar Creator gives you extensive templates and calendar backgrounds. Add a few photographs and you have a personalized calendar that makes a great holiday present.

You'll find many other programs to help with your printing projects, but before you run out and buy one, you need to check out a few things. First, see if you already have special printing software with your printer. Many manufacturers include this software with their printers when you purchase them.

Sometimes the programs that come with a printer are quite comprehensive. Although HP, Epson, Lexmark, and others come with good software, the Canon software is a personal favorite of mine. Most Canon printers come with several software programs. The Easy-PhotoPrint software for PC or Mac automatically boosts color saturation and eliminates photo noise, producing exceptionally vivid colors. It also automatically adjusts the size of the printer output so you can print that picture without a bit of hassle. Easy-PhotoPrint also lets you decide how many photos you want on a sheet, and prompts you to tell it the type and size of paper you are using so results are always excellent (see Figure 6.9) Did I mention that it is very intuitive and easy to use? It is by far the best photo-printing software I have seen.

The second included program is the Easy-WebPrint software. It is for Windows only and requires Internet Explorer 5.5 or better. This software automatically smoothes and formats web pages so they print properly. It resizes web pages to fit the standard printer page so they can be printed without losing information on the right side of the page as happens so often when you simply click on Print. Easy-WebPrint is easy to use and produces excellent results. This program is wonderful for printing web pages that can otherwise be cumbersome to print.

BLOOPER ALERT

Manufacturers are constantly changing their printers as well as their software lineup. If you are interested in one of the programs I mention here, make sure that it will come with the printer you purchase.

The PhotoRecord software, for Windows only, is basically for printing photo albums. The ZoomBrowser EX (Windows) and ImageBrowser (Mac) help you organize all your photos. The

PhotoStitch software works for Windows and Mac to make it easy to stitch together digital images shot in the panoramic mode. I used it to stitch together shots I had taken of the Alps and it worked beautifully.

FIGURE 6.9
Canon's Easy PhotoPrint software makes it easy to print photographs.

Have Fun with Your Printer

You might have purchased an inkjet printer to print photographs, but you can also use it for many other projects you might not have even considered when you made your printer purchase. Here are a few ways to turn your printer, paper, and ink into fun. You might even surprise yourself with your creativity!

You can give your photo printing a new twist in many ways. Why not take those precious pics and put them on a T-shirt, apron, or tote bag. Just purchase iron-on transfer paper that is specifically made for fabric.

Then print the image on the special paper. Be sure to follow the instructions, as the paper might require a reverse image. Next iron the image onto the fabric and voila, you've created a personalized masterpiece.

You can make your own newsletters, business cards, stationery, invitations, party favors, gift tags, recipe cards, CD labels, and photo frames, to name just a few. If you are very creative you can develop these on your own, but a good software program makes the job easier.

Printer manufacturer websites are also a great place to go for print project ideas, templates, and instructions. These are free for the taking and you can use any of these websites no matter what type of printer you own. Unfortunately, it can be difficult to find these helpful project sites from the manufacturer's main page.

The Canon Creative Park at http://bj.canon.co.jp/english has free greeting cards, clip art, a digital photo gallery, and a wealth of digital camera and printer tips. The extensive 3-D paper craft project area is well worth a look. You can print and build a farm diorama, games, and masks. There are projects that kids will love and adults will love to help with.

The HP Activity Center at http://h10050.www1.hp.com/activitycenter/us/en/ focuses on seasonal projects and holiday themes. They have many customizable projects such as photo frames and greeting cards, as shown in Figure 6.10. While you are there, be sure to look through the menu for other fun activities. The HP Scrapbooking site and the HP Quilting site are both fun to visit. The HP Activity Center offers hundreds of free print projects.

Epson also offers free print projects at Epson Print Labs (www.epson.com/cgi-bin/Store/PrintLab/PrintLab.jsp). You'll find projects to showcase your favorite photos, scrapbooking ideas, and patterned pages to print, as well as greeting cards, clip art, and seasonal projects. They also have an area called Cool School Tools. Even if you are not in school you might want to check these out. They include making creative hats, such as a nurse's cap, a pirate, and a bunny. I also enjoyed the fun project that shows you how to make designs that feature the American Flag, and the Fun with Frames section.

FIGURE 6.10
The HP Activity Center has instructions for many free printing projects.

I would be hard pressed to select the best of these three manufacturers' websites. They all have fun-filled projects, great templates, and all are free. Visit all three and you are sure to find some great ways to use your inkjet printer.

Other Options for Getting Photos Printed

If you don't want to print your own photographs, printing services can print your photos for you. In fact, there are so many wonderful photo service websites that choosing a site might be the hardest part of getting your photos printed. The most popular sites include

- **ClubPhoto**—www.clubphoto.com

- **ImageStation**—www.imagestation.com

- **Kodak EasyShare Gallery**—www.kodakgallery.com

- **PhotoWorks**—www.photoworks.com

- **Shutterfly**—www.shutterfly.com

- **Snapfish**—www.snapfish.com

Look for many things in a photo-printing website. You should judge a site on the value it provides for you. This is different for each user. You always want an attractive, intuitive user interface and an easy upload process. Of course, cost and quality of the prints is always important.

For most users, finding the right photo website is a trial-and-error experience. The good part is that it can really be fun to try different photo-printing sites. Most, even those with subscription fees, have some sort of free trial. Many sites entice would-be subscribers with free 4" × 6" photo prints. So you can often get free prints while you try different services.

If you are a Mac user and you work with iPhoto to edit and organize your photos, you can also purchase bound albums and other photo products printed directly from your albums in iPhoto. See iPhoto's Help feature for more details on how to get printed products through iPhoto.

LINGO

Digitizing simply means putting in digital format. A scanner will take an old photo and transfer it to the computer in digital form.

Restoring Old Photos

If, like me, you happen to have boxes and boxes of old photographs, digitizing them can be a fun project. You will need a scanner to scan the photos into the computer and software to help restore them if they are faded, scratched, or damaged. Don't fret. Technology has you covered. With the current crop of scanners and software, this project is easy.

Restoring Photos

You can use one of the many photo-editing programs available to restore your old photos after you've scanned them in with a scanner. Or you can choose a scanner that will restore them for you.

sandy's tip
If you have 35mm film or old slides to digitize, make sure that the scanner can handle that particular type of media.

The newer scanners also make it easy to scan 35mm film strips and slides. In the past you had to purchase a special expensive slide or film adapter and an expensive scanner to accommodate film or slides, but all that has changed. Many of the newer scanners from Epson, Canon, HP, and others are inexpensive and they have the built-in capability to handle film and slides.

My first granddaughter was born just about the time that these new scanners first appeared. Being proud grandparents, we took a ton of digital photos. I then dragged out my old family photos to show my daughter how much the baby looked like her. Compared to the new photos, the thirty-year-old ones looked scratched, dull, and drab. So I took a few and scanned them into the computer. The scanner's software automatically removed the scratches, spots, and dust particles. It also brightened the old images. It was even able to automatically remove the white border on the old photos. The results were so outstanding that I have now started a new project to scan my old photos into the computer and store them on CDs. Not only will I have my old photos preserved, but they will look better than ever.

All this magic was performed by the scanner with the help of the included software. This hardware/software combination worked flawlessly with my old photos. Some of photographs had deteriorated so much that I couldn't even determine the color of the person's clothing. When scanned in using the restoration software, the colors were clear and natural looking.

The scanner that I was working with at that time was a Canon CanoScan LiDE80. That scanner has been replaced by a newer version, but I am

Sandy's tip
With some scan-
ners you have to feed
slides individually. If you
have a lot of slides to digitize, you can save yourself
some time and effort by
purchasing a scanner that
allows you to feed in several slides at a time.

sure that the quality and functionality has only
increased. Since then I have also tried Epson and
HP scanners that also magically restore old photos.

Learning Can Be Fun

Spend some time with your photo software to
learn how to manipulate your photographs. Not
only should you be able to use your software to
lighten, darken, and remove red eye, but you
should also investigate the functions that allow
you to crop the photos and adjust the size so they
print correctly.

The same goes for working with printing and scanning. It will take time,
patience, and an initial monetary investment in paper and ink to be able
to produce good photographs on your inkjet printer. In order to scan
and restore old photos you will have to learn to use the scanner and
software. You will, however, be rewarded with great photos without a
dark room or photo-processing fees.

Whether you are a real shutterbug, you are trying to display your creativity, you are creating family keepsakes, or you are restoring old photos, the new world of digital cameras, printers, and scanners makes it
easy.

Sandy's Summary

As a Girl Scout I earned a photography badge and have been hooked on photography ever since. This is one hobby that has changed dramatically over the years. The elimination of film and film processing costs make photography more affordable than ever before. Being able to view your photographs immediately means you can correct your mistakes and become a better photographer with ease.

On top of that, digital photography gives you the fun of being able to see your photos right after you take them. You can print them immediately or email them to family and friends quickly and easily. I recently went to a family wedding in Chicago and emailed pictures of the event to my daughter in Sweden the same day. It doesn't get much better than that!

Digital photography is different than traditional photography, so there is some new terminology to learn. You also have to learn a little about resolution, file formats, memory cards, and batteries. Yet, digital photography is worth investing a little time to learn. It allows you to capture those precious memories for all to see.

Using an inkjet printer enables you to print your photos at home. Special software has been created to help you edit your photos and prepare them for printing. After you learn how to use this software, you will be amazed at what you can do with your computer and digital photographs. If you haven't yet purchased a digital camera, read this chapter, and then jump right in. If you are already a part of the digital photography world, keep on snapping those pictures. The next masterpiece is in the making.

Sandy Berger

Chapter 7

Music, Games, and Digital Diversions

"A hobby a day keeps the doldrums away."

—Phyllis McGinley

W hat's your passion? Music? Cooking? Gardening? Bird-watching? Whatever it is, there are hundreds of websites, resources, and others who share your interests online. The Internet and today's new gadgets and gizmos can help you have more fun with your hobbies and enable you to share them with others. With these wonderful high-tech resources you might even find a new pastime. In any case, these digital tools are sure to make your leisure pursuits more pleasurable.

The Magical World of Digital Music

If you are a music lover, you might have already found that computers can make beautiful music.

Sandy's tip
When purchasing speakers for your computer, be sure to buy magnetically shielded speakers because unshielded speakers might cause interference on your monitor or other computer devices.

Just a few short years ago, a beep was the only sound most computers could make. Times certainly have changed. Today computers often come with speakers and CD-ROM drives. Some even come with subwoofers. These components turn your computer into a full-fledged stereo system. Advances in digital audio technology have paired music and computers in an inseparable way.

Playing Music on Your Computer

If you don't have a set of good computer speakers, you can purchase them quite inexpensively. As with stereo equipment, you can spend as little or as much as you want on speakers. Today, virtually all the new computers come with either a CD-ROM or a DVD drive. Either of these two drives can play music CDs.

Not only can you play CDs on your computer, you can also play digital music. Digital music can be recorded in several different formats. The most popular format is MP3. This is the type of digital music that most youngsters have become experts at using. While some of us in the older generation have just gotten used to Walkman portable music players, they now have tiny devices to play digital music that has been downloaded from a computer. These are often called MP3 players.

With digital audio technology, more than four hours of music will take up only about 250MB of hard disk space on a computer or portable music player. Since MP3 music is completely digital and downloadable, you don't even need a CD to play it. Simply download your favorite music from the Internet and play it back on your computer. MP3-compressed music has the same audio quality as the original recording format.

If you are using a computer with the Windows operating system, your computer has a program called Windows Media Player (see Figure 7. 1) that can be used to play digital music. This program makes downloading music from the Internet very easy. It also helps you organize and play all your digital media, whether it's your favorite music, videos, pictures, or recorded TV.

You can also burn your own music to CDs with this program. With just a few clicks, you can use Windows Media Player to set up an entire library of music and listen to it anytime you like. For more information about Windows Media Player, including where to download the latest version of the program, visit Microsoft's website at www.microsoft.com.

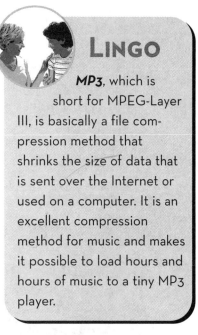

LINGO

MP3, which is short for MPEG-Layer III, is basically a file compression method that shrinks the size of data that is sent over the Internet or used on a computer. It is an excellent compression method for music and makes it possible to load hours and hours of music to a tiny MP3 player.

FIGURE 7.1
Windows Media Player is the music player that comes with the Windows operating system.

Just as Windows Media Player is the music player that comes on all Windows computers, iTunes is the free music player that comes with Apple computers (see Figure 7.2). iTunes is a great program that works similarly to Windows Media Player. Besides being a digital jukebox, iTunes also contains an iTunes Music Store where you can purchase more than 1.5 million digital songs. Apple users cannot use Windows Media Player, but Windows users can use iTunes. iTunes can be downloaded for free at www.apple.com/itunes. It has a great interface and I think that it is easier to use than Windows Media Player. So if you are a Windows user and you find that you don't like Windows Media Player, you can use iTunes instead.

FIGURE 7.2

iTunes, the popular music player that comes with the Mac operating system, is also available for the PC.

In fact, PC users have several free music players they can try. RealPlayer is available at www.real.com. Musicmatch Jukebox is available at www.musicmatch.com (see Figure 7.3). Winamp can be downloaded at www.winamp.com. All of these players have free versions. Versions you pay for come with additional features. Each of these music players is designed to play music, but all have diverse features and each looks and acts slightly differently.

BLOOPER ALERT

Some of the music sites that have free music players will try to sell you a pricey "pro" or "plus" version. You often have to scour their website to find the free version. Don't be tricked into the paid version when you really want the free version.

Portable Music Players

If you do want to take your music with you, a variety of portable music players are available today. They are some of the hottest devices around. In fact choosing a music player can be as difficult as choosing a shampoo. Head down the hair-care aisle of any drug store and you are sure to be overwhelmed by the choice of shampoos. Portable music players are no different. There is a large variety of devices, differing in size, weight, capacity, color, and sound quality.

FIGURE 7.3

At the Musicmatch website you can get a free music player as well as purchase music.

Portable music players attach to the computer by standard computer connections (typically a USB-type plug). You then use the software that comes with the music player to transfer music from your computer to the music player. You can copy a music CD you already own to your computer or use an online music service to purchase music and then download it to your music player.

The Apple iPod (www.ipod.com) has quickly become the star of digital music players. Its clean design, solid construction, large capacity, good sound quality, and long battery life have made it very popular. The easy control buttons make the iPod seem down-to-earth. When the iPod first appeared, it was available only for Apple computers. Now iPods can also be used with PCs. Over the years Apple has introduced a number of iPod types. They come in all sorts of sizes, colors, and capacities. You can get more information at the iPod website, shown in Figure 7.4.

FIGURE 7.4
The iPod website tells you all you need to know about this popular portable music player.

Other music players are available from a large variety of manufacturers. Here are just a few:

- **Creative Labs**—www. creative.com
- **Dell**—www.dell.com/electronics
- **iRiver**— www.iriver.com
- **Samsung**— www.samsung.com
- **Sony**—www.sony.com

When choosing a portable music player, consider size, weight, capacity, battery life, and sound quality. Also consider the online music services with which the player is compatible. For instance, the iPod music player is only compatible with the iTunes music service. Other players cannot use the iTunes website for purchasing music, but are able to download music at other websites.

Some things to consider when purchasing a portable music player are

✓ **Size**—Smaller can be better for portability, but make sure the controls are large enough to handle easily.

✓ **Weight**—Music players keep getting lighter and lighter. This is a big plus for portability.

✓ **Capacity**—This is usually measured in MB (megabytes) or GB (gigabytes). A 4GB music player holds approximately 1,000 songs.

✓ **Sound quality**—Everyone's ears are different. If you can, listen to the music player before you buy to see how it sounds to you.

✓ **Battery life**—The longer the battery lasts, the better. Most music players have rechargeable batteries. If you plan on keeping it for a long time, you might want to find out if the rechargeable battery is replaceable since it will eventually wear out, especially with heavy use.

✓ **Design**—Music players come in a large variety of shapes and sizes. You might prefer a different shape if you want to strap it to your arm while you are working out than you would choose if you want to carry it in your pocket.

✓ **Screen**—If the player has a screen, it should be large enough and clear enough to be easily seen. The screens are generally used to choose what song(s) you want to play at any given time. Some players such as the iPod shuffle have no screen; they simple play the music in a random order.

✓ **Compatible music websites**—Some music players can only be used to purchase music from certain web services. For instance, with an iPod you can only download music from Apple's iTunes online music store.

When choosing a portable music player, Mac users have it easy. They will most likely purchase an iPod made by Apple and use the iTunes music store also created by Apple. It is more complicated for PC users. Because of the large variety of music players and online music stores, PC users can often purchase a music player only to find that it might not work with the online music store they want to use to download music. For that reason, Microsoft has initiated a new testing and labeling scheme. The blue triangular PlaysForSure logo, shown in Figure 7.5, is put on portable music players and on online music stores that are compatible.

FIGURE 7.5
Look for the Microsoft PlaysForSure logo on a portable music player and on a music website to ensure compatibility.

Purchasing Music Online

I can remember sitting in the living room listening to my dad play "How Much Is That Doggie in the Window?" on our old record player. We could choose the music we wanted to hear rather than having to listen to whatever was played on the radio. After the record player was accepted into mainstream America, the 8-track player and cassette tapes made music more portable. When CDs entered the scene we got better quality. Now we have it all: the music of our choice, portability, and great sound quality. On top of all that, we can now purchase music without leaving home.

Sandy's tip
You don't have to purchase new music for your music player; you can simply copy your CDs to the computer and transfer that music to the music player.

Downloading songs from the Internet is revolutionizing the music industry. If you haven't tried it yet, you should. It's easy and it's fun. Whether you listen to Smashing Pumpkins or Tony Bennett, there is a musical genre for everyone.

Here's how it works. You choose a music download site to use. Then you download the software (if necessary) and peruse the available music (most sites let you listen to a clip of the music before you purchase). Then simply select the song(s) you want to download. You supply a credit card number and set up an account. Then you download the music to your computer. After the music is on your computer you can listen to it, copy it to a music player, or burn it to a CD.

Music can be purchased by the song, so you don't have to buy an entire album just to get the title song. Like music players, online music services vary greatly in price, ease-of-use, and amount and variety of available music.

Here are a few of the most popular music sites; check them out to decide which you like the best:

- **BuyMusic**—www.buymusic.com

- **iTunes**—www.itunes. com

- **Music Match**—www. musicmatch.com

- **Napster**—www.napster. com

- **Rhapsody**—www. rhapsody.com

- **Wal-Mart**—http:// musicdownloads.walmart.com

Each of these websites charges different prices for their songs and albums. So be sure to check the prices as well.

Digital Rights Management

Digital rights management is a complex issue. *Digital rights* deal with how many times you are allowed to copy the music, how many computers you can store it on, and just what rights you have as the purchaser of the music. Each music site might have different digital rights. Most allow you to store songs on up to three computers and transfer them to portable music players. Some limit the number of times you can burn a play list to a CD. For the most part, these restrictions don't interfere with the normal use of the music. If, however, you know you will want to make a lot of copies, and/or use your downloads on more than three computers, read the restrictions on the website before you purchase.

Trivia

Napster started as a free music file-sharing website that was forced to close. The new Napster is a legitimate music service that now charges for music.

Blooper Alert

Some online music services allow you to download all the music you want for a small monthly fee. The catch is that after you stop paying the monthly fee, the music you have downloaded is no longer available to you.

Radio with a New Twist

Once upon a time, owning a radio was a status symbol. My, how things have changed! Fast forward to today when most American homes have televisions, stereos, and CD players. Even the most inventive minds could not have imagined these technologies 70 years ago. Yet, even with these other somewhat superior technologies, radio has endured. Radio, with its mediocre quality and its tendency to hiss and crack, is still a mainstay in audio programming and transmissions.

Trivia

The radio gets it name from the word *radiation*. Radio transmissions are electromagnetic radiation (energy) that is sent through the air.

Developing rapidly from its early pre-1900s beginnings, radio quickly became our world's first mass medium. The radio became a means of disseminating information instantly from one person to many. Radio was a technology that influenced our growth as a nation and planet. Radio continues to be prominent as it uses technology to improve in unusual ways. If listening to the radio is one of your favorite pastimes, you're in luck. Technology is making radio better than ever before.

Satellite Radio

Remember taking a road trip in the "good old days?" As soon as you left the big city, you lost the radio station you were listening to. You spent the rest of the trip adjusting the radio to find the best station in the area you were passing through. Well, satellite radio has made that scenario a thing of the past. With satellite radio you can start at the Eastern seaboard and drive to the California coast listening to the same radio station with near perfect reception. Even better, you have your choice of more than 100 music, sports, news, and entertainment channels (or *streams* as they are called in the satellite world). The streams are varied and are of excellent quality. Just about every music genre is covered, including pop, rock, country, hip hop, R&B, dance, jazz, classical, and variety. Most of the stations are commercial-free or have very few commercials.

The magic is created by satellites in high-angle elliptical orbits over the United States. In order to listen you need a special radio receiver and you must also pay a monthly fee. Two competing satellite services are now in place: Sirius at www.sirius.com (see Figure 7.6) and XM Radio at www.xmradio.com. Satellite radio has become a popular option that can be pre-installed on most new cars. In general, the make of the car you choose will determine whether you get Sirius or XM radio service. Unfortunately, at the present time the receivers used by Sirius and XM are not compatible.

FIGURE 7.6
The Sirius satellite radio website will give you information on the company as well as a programming line-up.

You can also purchase satellite radio receivers for your home, office, or boat. They are portable units that can be used almost anywhere. Some satellite receivers can be used in the car and then taken inside the home or office. Many are portable and small enough to hold in

Trivia

In just a few years, XM satellite radio has garnered more than 4 million subscribers.

your hand. Some allow you to record the satellite radio programming and then play it back anytime, anywhere.

Sandy's tip

You might want to choose your satellite radio company based on the programming. Each has a different lineup. This is especially true of sports. One satellite network will have the baseball programming while the other might focus on basketball or football.

If you think that satellite radio is just for kids, think again. There is plenty of programming targeted at Boomers and Zoomers. From old time radio shows to Frank Sinatra, there is plenty to like. You can listen to the music of the 40s, 50s, and so on. Special programming, such as a Tribute to Dean Martin Weekend, is always on tap on either satellite radio service.

Digital Radio

Satellite radio services aspire to assault broadcast radio like cable has battered broadcast television. Broadcast radio has poised to counterattack with a move to digital transmissions. Digital radio eliminates static, hissing, and popping. It improves fidelity so much that AM radio sounds better than the current FM transmissions, and FM radio offers CD-quality audio. iBiquity Digital Corporation has developed a technology that allows digital radio signals to ride the same airwaves as analog AM/FM radio.

After the listener purchases a digital receiver that pulls in the digital signal, this technology brings in clear digital sound to current and future radio stations. Since additional information can travel along with the digital data, radio listeners have access to local traffic conditions, weather, and other information that can be displayed on the digital receiver along with the song title. This technology piggybacks on the analog signal so existing radios will continue to receive the analog signals while the new radio receiver receives both analog and digital signals. Stations will continue to be found at their current locations on the dial. For more information on digital radio, visit the iBiquity (www.ibiquity.com) website shown in Figure 7.7.

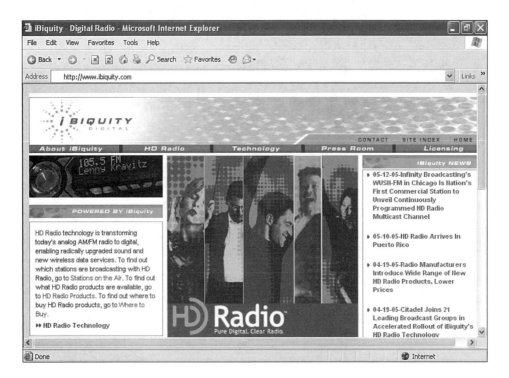

FIGURE 7.7
The iBiquity website will tell you all about digital radio.

Old Hobbies, New Tools

After reading Chapter 6, "Digital Photography and Instant Printing," you know that digital cameras have transformed photography into a more affordable hobby that can be enjoyed by all. With instant results and no additional film or development costs, learning how to be a great photographer is easier than ever before.

Technology has infiltrated many traditional hobbies, turning them into digital diversions. Remember when your grandmother used to sew things by hand or use the foot pedals to power her sewing machine? Times sure are changing! Now even sewing machines have gone digital. Bernina (www.bernina.com), one of the world's largest and oldest sewing machine companies, has introduced a line of computerized sewing machines, called Artista. These machines are powered by a special version of the Microsoft Windows operating system called Windows CE. This computer power gives the machines the ability to sew more than 850 types of stitches. They have a color touch screen for access to features. With an optional modem, the machines can download embroidery designs, access updated sewing tips, and navigate through Bernina's premium content. This sewing machine is so advanced that it can remember the last 15 stitches used even after the machine is turned off.

Computers, printers, scanners, and digital cameras have also revolutionized the old hobby of scrapbooking. If you want a background paper to frame your photos, you can simply print it on your inkjet printer. Old photos can be scanned into the computer and revitalized. Photos can be given special effects with a photo-editing program, or they can be printed on special paper, fabric, or canvas using an inkjet printer. Even the little things about scrapbooking have been transformed with high-tech products, such as special glue that allows photos and trimmings to be easily repositioned.

Although paper-based scrapbooking is still very popular, some scrapbookers are now creating completely digital scrapbooks. Digital photos are framed with borders and flourishes right on the computer screen. Text is embellished with unique fonts and special computer-created word art. Completed digital books can be printed or shared online or by email.

The Internet also lends a hand when it comes to creating fantastic memory books. For layouts, projects, and ideas, head over to *Scrapbooking.com Magazine* at www.scrapbooking.com (see Figure 7.8). For a slightly different approach to scrapbooking, try Scrapjazz at www.scrapjazz.com. It has product reviews, message boards, and just about everything you ever wanted to know about scrapbooking. If you are just getting in to scrapbooking, surf over to Scrapbooking 101 at www.scrapbooking101.net. It is filled with great information about basic techniques, as well as the latest and greatest scrapbooking trends.

Several great scrapbooking software programs help you lay out pages, edit pictures, create collages, add frames, and create albums. Here are a few to choose from:

- **Art Explosion Scrapbook Factory by Nova**— www.novadevelopment.com

- **Creating Keepsakes by Broderbund**—www.broderbund.com

- **My Scrapbook by Ulead**—www.ulead.com/mse

- **Hallmark Scrapbook Studio by Sierra**—www.sierrahome.com

FIGURE 7.8
Scrapbooking.com is an online scrapbooking magazine.

Whether your love is astronomy or zoology or anything in between, the Internet is ready to give you guidance and get your creative juices flowing. It can even connect you with others who share your hobby. Just enter the name of your hobby in any search engine and you are sure to find abundant resources.

If you are looking for a new hobby or want to check out the latest trends, visit the National Craft Association at www.craftassoc.com. For hobby and craft supplies, try eHobbies at www.ehobbies.com or HobbyWorld at www.hobby-world.com. Whether it's model railroading, butterfly collecting, knitting, or cooking, the Internet proves to be an invaluable resource once again.

Exciting New Diversions

The nifty thing about the Internet is that its existence has created new hobbies. So if you want to plunge into the digital world, try an exciting new hobby such as geocaching or blogging. Sound like something from the Star Trek Enterprise? The sections that follows will explain these new hobbies and more. You might even get you curious enough to try one.

Geocaching

This exciting new hobby is a takeoff of an old game. Geocaching is a new high-tech form of the treasure hunt. While it is also similar to the game of hide-and-seek, it is even more reminiscent of the well-loved scavenger hunts most of us played when we were growing up. Instead of faded maps and handwritten instructions, this game uses a high-tech device called a Global Positioning System (GPS) to search for hidden treasures. The GPS navigator uses satellite technology to pinpoint an exact location anywhere on the planet. A large variety of GPS devices are available. Geocachers are generally use small handheld devices. Some cost less than $100. Models that include built-in maps, compasses, and voice navigation can cost more than $1,000.

Trivia

The GPS satellite system was designed by and is controlled by the U.S. Department of Defense. It can now be used free of charge by anyone. The first GPS satellite was placed into orbit in 1989.

There are several variations to this game, but all are essentially the same. People hide the treasure which is called a *cache* (pronounced *cash*). They document the exact latitude and longitude of the cache they have hidden by entering that information on the Internet at websites such as www.geocaching.com, shown in Figure 7.9. Start the game by visiting a geocaching website and getting the location of a cache in the area where you want to play. Then use your GPS device to find the cache.

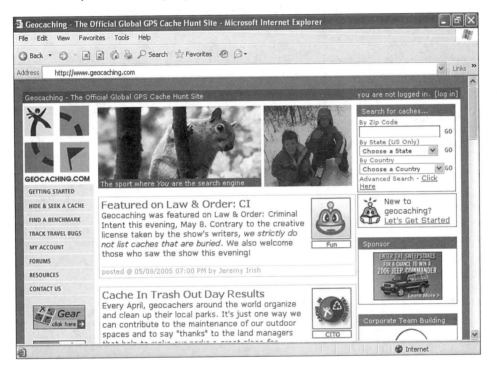

FIGURE 7.9
Geocaching.com is one place to start enjoying this exciting new sport.

It sounds easy, but it can be very challenging. The GPS will get you to the correct longitude and latitude, but you still have to find the treasure yourself. The cache might be hidden inside a building, underwater, or on the side of a rocky cliff. Sometimes you can see the location that the GPS indicates, but there might be an immovable object such as a lake or hill that you must circumnavigate to get to the treasure. Part of the game is to hide the cache in some unusual or difficult-to-reach spot to add to the thrill of the hunt.

Trivia

The treasure in geocaching is called a cache. Cache is also a computer term that refers to a part of the computer's memory that is usually unseen or hidden from the computer user.

To continue the game you are expected to rebury the same cache or use a new one. Because the cache is often exposed to the elements, it is generally put in a plastic or other type of waterproof container. It almost always contains a log book that was left by the person who first hid the cache. That book is signed by all the people who have found the treasure. Besides the log book, the cache can contain trinkets, games, and pictures. Some well-to-do folks have made a sport of putting various amounts of real cash into the cache. This, plus the thrill of the hunt, has made geocaching a sport that has spread to all 50 states and hundreds of different countries.

Treasures are everywhere. Although I live in a small town in North Carolina, when I entered my ZIP code at geocaching.com, I found that there were 24 hidden caches within 10 miles of my home. Entering a ZIP code for suburban New York revealed 267 caches in a 10-mile radius.

If you liked playing hide-and-seek when you were a kid, why not try this new high-tech game? For more information on how to get started, check out Geocaching.com (www.geocaching.com) and Navicache (www.navicache.com). Then get out there. This is a classic sport that has used technology to re-create itself. You can get some exercise and fresh air and have fun at the same time!

Blogging

Another new and exciting digital diversion and one of the latest high-tech fads is blogging. Blogging is writing a personal journal that is publicly accessible on the Web. There are thousands of blogs on the Web, from political blogs to travel blogs. Just reading the blogs of others can become a substantial pastime. Yet many people are now creating and updating blogs as a kind of digital hobby. This new type of journalism allows everyone to be a writer and to publish their work on the Web.

Since there are no editors or publishers involved, the author can maintain complete control.

You don't need any technical expertise to create a blog. Blogging software and built-in tools make creating blogs easy. The best place to start might be the free Blogger software available from Google at www.blogger.com, shown in Figure 7.10. This software is easy to use. It performs basic blogging functions and also has plenty of additional features, such as the capability to post pictures and get comments from readers.

LINGO

The word **blog** is short for *weblog*. Blogs are a form of journaling on the Internet that can be anything from someone's personal diary to chronicling the evolution of someone's business or some event.

FIGURE 7.10
Using Blogger.com is one of the easiest ways to create a blog.

Other blogging software is available from companies such as TypePad at www.typepad.com, pMachine at www.pmachine.com, and Moveable Type at www.sixapart.com/movabletype.

If you have always wanted to be a journalist, you like to write letters to the editor in your local newspaper, or you have thoughts and feelings you would like to share with others, check out the idea of blogging. It might be for you!

Webcamming

LINGO

A **webcam** is a camera that allows viewing of live images through the Internet.

Another digital creation you are likely to love is the webcam, shown in Figure 7.11. You will be amazed at this nifty little device's ability to enable you to see your grandson opening his birthday presents or your niece playing her new clarinet. Whether they are across town or halfway around the world, webcams allow you to see live action. Most webcams are equipped with a myriad options, such as a digital zoom, built-in microphone, and motion sensor. You can use it to send videos or photos in your email, use it for live video chats with your friends and family, set it up as a video monitoring system, send live video to mobile phones, create movies, and even post videos to websites.

Sandy's tip

If you are using AOL's Instant Messenger, Yahoo!'s Messenger, iChat, or Windows Messenger, you can add live images to your instant messages with a webcam.

Webcams provide a great way to enjoy a picture-phone connection with your family and friends. What a great way to share hobbies, participate in parties and celebrations, or watch a baby's first steps.

FIGURE 7.11
A webcam can provide hours of enjoyment.

Old Hobbies Get New Life

Don't think that only new hobbies are now high tech. Technology has injected new life into many favorite old hobbies. From gardening to sewing to gaming, new techniques and Internet resources are transforming classic hobbies, making them more fun than ever before.

Classic Car Lovers

Even some of the oldest hobbies, such as the love of cars, are benefiting from technology. While classic car lovers are interested in classics, the high-tech Internet is still helping them with their hobby. Classic car aficionados are logging many miles over the Internet using websites that offer them research, clubs, chat rooms, and information about classic car events.

Hemmings at www.hemmings.com is a great place for vehicle enthusiasts to visit a car show, look up the value of a specific model, and check out the abandoned auto of the week.

The Internet also provides access to many special interest auto clubs that revolve around a specific make or model. For instance, The Packard Club (see Figure 7.12), located at www.packardclub.org, is dedicated to preserving the products and history of the Packard Motor Car Company. Other online clubs have formed for general interests and fellowship. Membership often includes organized trips, social events, and monthly club magazines and newsletters. Members gather online to find show listings, get technical tips, and to buy and sell cars and related items.

Antique car lovers have Internet resources that are too extensive to list here, but if you are a car buff, don't miss Kruse International (www.kruseinternational.com), the largest auction company for collector cars. Also be sure to visit Classic Car.com (www.classiccar.com) and My ClassicCar.com (www.myclassiccar.com). Both have great pictures, information, and tutorials. Even if you are not an antique car lover, just looking at all these grand stylish iron horses at these websites might give you a touch of the classic car fever.

Internet Gourmet

There are websites galore for anything and everything related to food, from preparing it, to consuming it, to purchasing it online.

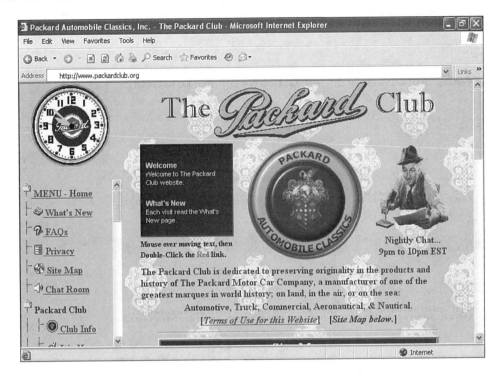

FIGURE 7.12
The Packard Club is just one of many online special interest groups formed by antique car lovers.

Whether you are a food connoisseur or a novice cook, you will want to check out Epicurious (www.epicurious.com), which boasts of having "the world's greatest recipe collection," and also includes online versions of the *Bon Appétit* and *Gourmet* magazines. The Epicurious site offers many great recipes, monthly food columns, and menus for nearly every occasion you can think of, from midsummer barbeques to wine country menus.

If you need last-minute help to get that Thanksgiving, Christmas, or family gathering feast just right, check out AllRecipes at www.allrecipes.com for a cornucopia of recipes, menu ideas, cooking hints, and planning tips. For picture-perfect and stress-free food ideas and how-tos, you'll find no less than 25,000 recipes, as well as a recipe of the day. An online recipe clipboard keeps up with your most recently viewed recipes that you can bookmark for easy retrieval when you want to see them again. There's even an online community for home cooks where you can share your favorite recipes. AllRecipes claims to have the "world's largest community of home cooks with over 10 million" users.

For the vegetarian, www.vegsoc.org is a superb website. The Vegetarian Society, shown in Figure 7.13, claims to be the oldest vegetarian society in the world. They offer nutritional advice and instructions on how to cook for vegetarians. Whether you are a confirmed vegan or are just interested in getting nutritious recipes and food facts, you'll want to check out this website.

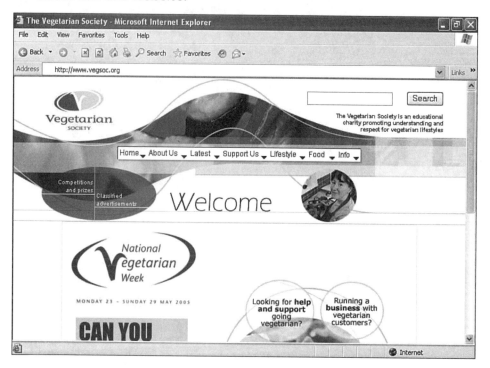

FIGURE 7.13
The Vegetarian Society website has information for everyone.

You can also visit your local grocery stores online. Whole Foods, which has store locations scattered throughout North America and the United Kingdom, also has a website at www.wholefoods.com. This unique food retailer specializes in natural and organic foods. From its website, you can research the types of food it sells, read articles about health and nutrition, search for a store location near you, and get recipes. Participating stores offer catering with choices including their signature items such as Greek Crostini and Sesame Ginger Flank Steak. Whole Foods will also bring the flowers and the wine.

For online food shopping, visit www.netgrocer.com. Regardless of your ZIP code, NetGrocer can deliver just about anything you normally buy at the local grocer. Inside this online store is a grocery store for items such as cereal, laundry products, meats, vegetables, pet supplies, and international foods. There is a drug store for cough and cold items, nutritional supplements, and personal care. Included is a general store with cameras, film, office products, and toys. You can also purchase natural and organic foods and products, as well as kosher foods. NetGrocer ships your groceries via Federal Express to all of the continental United States. They also ship to men and women in the foreign service who work abroad.

Blooming As an Internet Gardener

There are literally thousands of websites devoted to gardening providing you with an endless supply of information on growing anything and everything. The Internet supplies you with a full crop of plant encyclopedias, garden designs and plans, how-tos, weather zone maps, and gardening tips, as well as garden-specific message boards and chat rooms. Just about any information you are willing to dig up or harvest is available on the Web.

To take your first look at the spectacular resources available through the Internet, type the word *gardening* into any search engine and you will find an overwhelming list of links. Whether you are looking for garden supplies or information on container gardening, you'll find plenty of information to sort through.

Gardening Websites

If you want to go directly to several gardening websites, type **www.rebeccasgarden.com** into the address bar of your Internet browser. Rebecca Kolls will hold your hand at Rebecca's Garden, shown in Figure 7.14. Visit Rebecca's Garden for step-by-step gardening instructions and plenty of quick tips.

FIGURE 7.14
Rebecca's Garden is filled with information for the nature lover.

A great site called the GardenWeb describes itself as the "Internet's garden community." The web address for this popular site is www.gardenweb.com. GardenWeb stands apart by being the first to have established an actual community of users through web forums. GardenWeb hosts garden exchanges, articles, contests, and a large botanical glossary with more than 4,000 entries. GardenWeb's HortiPlex Plant Database offers plant images and data as well as links to information sources and vendors. An interesting feature is the Garden Exchange where gardeners post requests for seeds and plants as well as offers of items for trade. Other links whisk you off to a calendar of events and directories of nurseries, catalogs, gardening societies and associations, and cooperative extension services.

Trees and Birds and Bees

A visit to www.arborday.org, the National Arbor Day Foundation's website, makes selecting trees for your climate as easy as snapping your fingers. Go to the site's online tree store, type in your ZIP code, and find out which trees thrive in your area. Be sure to check for recommendations on tree care before leaving this site. You can also find out about topping (that is *no* topping, mind you), pruning, making cuts, using mulch, and planting containerized trees. Free trees are even available if you are willing to become a foundation member.

The National Wildlife Federation can help you make your lawn hospitable to wildlife. Visit this website at www.nwf.org. Their Backyard Wildlife Habitat Program will make you a more alert and informed watcher of butterflies and hummingbirds as they flit and fly through the air. You'll be paying more attention to frogs and lizards as they dance through your yard. This interactive site can be invaluable for planning and improving your outdoor habitat. Sign up for its monthly e-newsletter to stay informed on what is going on in the world of wildlife.

Organic Gardening

What does it take to be an organic gardener? For one thing, you have to steer clear of synthetic fertilizers and pesticides and pay close attention to your soil. At OrganicGardening.com (see Figure 7.15) you will find an extensive organic-oriented site to help you organize a garden that blooms nearly year round. It tells you how to get your soil tested and gets you started growing perennial and carefree vegetables. If you want simple instructions and helpful hints for sowing and tending your own seedlings indoors and organically, visit www.organicgardening.com.

FIGURE 7.15
Focusing on all natural resources, the Organic Gardening website is brimming with information.

Herb Gardening

For a wealth of information on herb gardening, www.herbgardening.com boasts that it provides "everything you need to know about growing herbs." At HerbGardening.com you will find step-by-step herb gardening guides, information on planting and caring for herbs, how to grow them indoors, and even recipes. Another resourceful website is GardenGuides. After you become familiar with this site, you will very likely decide to visit it often. The web address is www.gardenguides.com. Click on the Herb Guide link to get started on becoming an herb-gardening expert. This site has some interesting information on herbs, including which ones are perennial, biennial, and annual. It also shares valuable information on vegetables and flowers, and a forum enables you to interact with others concerning your gardening questions and comments.

If your Web workout is taking away your time and energy from the spade, trowel, and hose, don't despair. After that sunshine is on your back and your fingers are in the soil, your love for the garden will take over. Your new knowledge of perennials and annuals, herbs, organic gardening, garden designs, and soil content will bloom, literally speaking, into an enchanting garden spot—thanks to your gardener's love and energy...and your Internet connection.

Games Galore

The variety of games on the Internet is almost overwhelming. Although the younger generation might be going wild over the shoot-'em-up games, the older crowd is finding a wealth of games that suit their tastes.

Computer Games

Go by any computer store and peruse the software section and you will find a plethora of games that can be played on your computer. Classic board games, such as Scrabble and Monopoly, have computerized versions. There are computer card games, fast-paced racing games, adventure games, and many, many more. Anyone who has ever played Solitaire on the computer knows that even the simplest computer games can be fun.

Computer games can bring enjoyment while helping you fulfill lifelong ambitions. If you've always wanted to fly an airplane, you can do it with a game such as Microsoft's Flight Simulator, which gives

Sandy's tip
Remember that games are operating-system specific. If you have a Windows PC, you will want to purchase games created for the Windows operating system. Mac users will buy games that were specifically created for the Mac.

BLOOPER ALERT
Before you buy a game, be sure to check out the system requirements. Because some games require a lot of computer power, you want to be sure your computer can handle the game before you make your purchase.

you a choice of airplanes, airports, weather conditions, and more. Race car simulation games such as the Nascar Racing series can give you the look and feel of actually driving the race car. You can even purchase a steering wheel and foot pads to make the game more realistic.

With the advanced graphics of today's computers, playing games on the computer can transport you to a visual wonderland. In fact, some of these games create their own world for you right in front of your eyes. Sims, the best-selling PC game, allows you to create entire cities. You can build and furnish your dream house. Create the characters to live in it and then go on to create an entire community. The Sims games (http://thesims.ea.com/us/) have been so popular that many different versions have been released. The Sims 2 game, shown in Figure 7.16, has very realistic graphics.

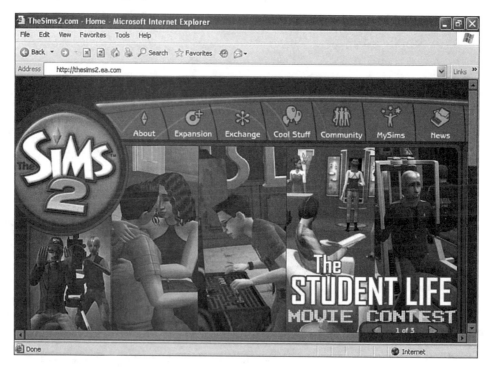

FIGURE 7.16
The Sims2 game has realistic animations.

There are so many computer games available that I couldn't even begin to tell you about them all in this book. There are adult-only games as well as many child-oriented games. Of course, there are also games that are suitable for all ages. One that I especially like for the whole family is Roller Coaster Tycoon (www.rollercoastertycoon.com). In the latest version you can not only create your own amusement park, but you can ride the roller coasters you create and light up the night sky with fireworks.

Online Gaming

Many computer games can be played alone, with family and friends, or with online partners and opponents. Interactive online gaming has quickly and quietly become one of the most popular entertainment categories in the United States. At any given time, hundreds of thousands of gamers are playing online. So if you happen to be awake at 3 a.m., you will not lack for company in an Internet game room.

You can play chess, checkers, Monopoly, or just about every other game you can imagine online. There are also many well-liked games that were created just for online play. EverQuest (www.everquest.com) is one of the most popular. This is a multiplayer role-playing adventure game that takes place in a wonderful, visually beautiful fantasy world. It is both exciting and addictive.

Sandy's tip

Be sure to read the terms of use and the privacy policy on any website before you download files.

There are several different payment scenarios for gaming on the Internet. Many games are free. Some charge to download the game to your computer. Some are offshoots of a retail game where you purchase a boxed game and play that game either alone, with your own friends, or online with others who also own the game. Some games, such as EverQuest, charge a monthly fee.

BLOOPER ALERT

Watch out; some game sites charge just for the privilege of playing and that can be expensive.

When playing games over the Internet, especially online games, connection speed can be important. Although playing over a regular dial-up connection is fun, communication delays and pauses can cause frustration in some games. Playing over a broadband connection, such as DSL or cable, is definitely preferable. If you have a slow Internet connection and don't like to tie up your telephone line, don't worry; many websites have download-able games you can play.

Not sure where you want to begin? Why not visit a few gaming web-sites to get you started? A popular game site where you can play online or download games is GameHouse at www.gamehouse.com. At GameHouse (see Figure 7.17) you can play games for free and you don't have to register at this site, although you can register if you want. You just surf over and start playing. Rules are provided for the games, and if you find a game you really like, you can pay a fee to download a super version of the game to your hard drive. The super version has addi-tional features, better graphics, improved sound, and gives you the abil-ity to play the game offline.

GameHouse has a large variety of excellent games that will appeal to Boomers and Zoomers. For instance, there is a grid-type game called Candy Cruncher, an extremely habit-forming game called Addiction Solitaire, and an intriguing word game called TextTwist. Mac users will be happy to find many of the games available for their computers, too. Several games are available for playing on a personal digital assistant such as a Palm Pilot.

Another popular game website is Yahoo! Games. Go to www.yahoo.com and click on the Games link. There you will find card games, board games, puzzles, word games, arcades, and much more. There are single-player games and games for multiple players. You can even join a backgammon tournament or a pinochle league.

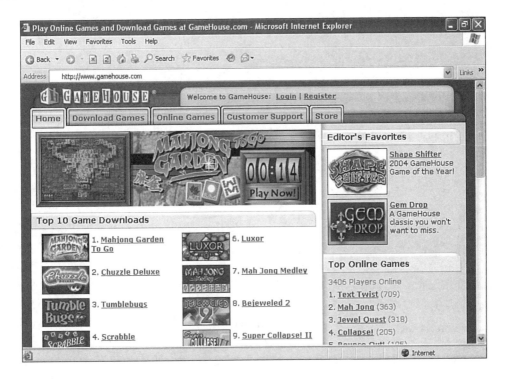

FIGURE 7.17
GameHouse has games you can play online or download to your computer.

If you search the Web you will find many free gaming sites. The MiniClip website (www.miniclip.com) has enough games to keep you busy for quite awhile.

Video Games for Grown-ups

You might think that video games are just for kids, but many Boomers and Zoomers also enjoy them. The three most popular video game consoles are

- **Sony PlayStation—** www.playstation.com

Sandy's tip
When looking for free games, don't just look at gaming websites. Many websites such as Compu-KISS (www. compukiss.com/ kissgamers/index.cfm) and AARP (www.aarp.org/fun) offer free games along with other information.

- **Nintendo GameCube**—www.gamecube.com
- **Microsoft Xbox**—www.xbox.com

All three hook up to your television and are similar in nature. You purchase the machine and then you purchase the games, which come on a small cartridge or CD.

Sandy's tip
Many game consoles such as the Xbox and PlayStation can be plugged in and played over the Internet for multiplayer games.

As the manufacturers of these devices are constantly competing, every version of each device gets better and better. You might purchase a certain game console because that is the one your children or grandchildren like and use. If, however, you are choosing a video game console for yourself, you should make your choice based on the available games. All of these devices have good shoot-'em-up games. But you might be more interested in sports or family-orientated games. See which devices have games for the sports in which you are interested. Don't worry, all of the sports are covered. There are games that feature everything from golf to hockey. If you are interested in family-orientated games, the Nintendo GameCube has a definite advantage with game series, such as Mario, Donkey Kong, and Kirby, that can be enjoyed by everyone. The Nintendo website with a picture of the GameCube is shown in Figure 7.18.

Handheld video games are also very popular. These have games similar to their big brothers systems that attach to the television. They have a small screen that enables them to be played without a television. The Sony PlayStation Portable (PSP) and the Nintendo Dual Screen (DS) are currently the two most popular handheld gaming devices.

FIGURE 7.18
Information about the Nintendo GameCube is available at the Nintendo website.

Games Are Good for Your Health

To keep your body in shape, you have to perform all those dreaded exercises and eat veggies instead of ice cream. To keep your mind in shape, all you have to do is play games. Research has shown that certain lifestyle regimens can keep your mind alert and can even lessen the risk of and forestall the onset of mind-changing diseases such as Alzheimer's and dementia. Activities that use problem-solving skills, such as working on puzzles or playing memory games, have been shown to

Sandy's tip
Age-related declines in mental ability affect 100% of the population. You can't escape, but you can make a difference. Use the computer and games to keep your mind active.

slow age-related declines in mental ability. Playing games can keep your mind active and sharpen you mentally.

Your physical body might also benefit from game playing. A recent article in NewScientist.com states, "Computer game players score off the charts in several standard vision tests...the visual skills of non-gamers improve dramatically after just 10 hours of playing action games."

Some doctors prepare for laproscopic surgery by playing fast-paced video games to improve their manual dexterity. So playing games might be more beneficial than you ever imagined.

Sandy's Summary

Computers and technology have changed our lives dramatically in the past few years. This is quite evident in entertainment and leisure activities. People all over the world are strapping small digital music players to their arms and plugging their ears with small earbuds that function like headphones. Downloading music from the Internet has become a major pastime that was unheard of just a few short years ago. Even traditional radio transmissions are moving to digital format, and satellite radio is already wildly popular.

Many traditional hobbies have been completely changed with digital tools. The digital camera has rocked the world of photography. Sewing machines have become computerized and even scrapbookers are going digital. At the same time, new high-tech hobbies such as geocaching and blogging are spreading like wildfire.

Almost all conventional hobbies, such as cooking, gardening, and even antique auto collecting, have been changed by the availability of Internet resources. These resources make these activities more accessible and more enjoyable than ever before.

In talking about digital diversions, let's not forget gaming! Computer games are amazingly varied and realistic. Online gaming is extremely popular. Video games are available for the whole family to play. On top of all that, research is now showing that playing digital games can be healthy.

Yes, technology has changed the world of leisure pursuits. So jump in and join the fun!

Sandy Berger

Chapter 8

Online Health Information and Resources

Age does not depend upon years, but upon temperament and health. Some men are born old, and some never grow so.

—Tryon Edwards

As we age, we quickly realize that we can't take good health for granted. Health is a state of complete well-being and not merely the absence of disease or infirmity.

The Internet is a great resource for health information. From eating right to researching disease, Internet resources will help you learn how to keep healthy and give you tools to find help when you are not. The Internet also serves as a good tool for tracking medical histories and reaching out to others who might suffer from similar ailments.

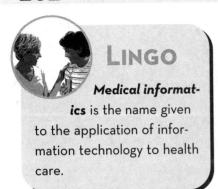

LINGO

Medical informatics is the name given to the application of information technology to health care.

Technology has greatly impacted medical procedures, disease control, and home health care. With new technology, you can check your blood pressure at home in seconds or swallow a pill containing a camera to avoid uncomfortable internal tests.

There is so much medical information provided by information technology that it's been given its own name—medical informatics.

Websites to Visit for Health and Medical Resources

Before the advent of the Internet, if the average person wanted to learn more about a disease or disorder, he would research it in a library, ask other people for advice, or make an appointment with his doctor. The information from the library often turned out to be dated. The advice from friends was not always accurate. The patient might have to wait weeks for an appointment with his doctor or with a specialist. The Internet has changed all that with excellent resources for information on health, fitness, and medicine.

Finding Medical Websites

If you are looking for general medical information on any specific topic, you can surf over to MedicineNet.com (www.medicinenet.com). MedicineNet.com is a network of physicians and health professionals that bring you the latest health news. WebMD (www.webmd.com) provides health information as well as tools for managing your health. WebMD has a wealth of data for medical information seekers. It can help you run through your symptoms to get a possible diagnosis and find a doctor when you need one (see Figure 8.1).

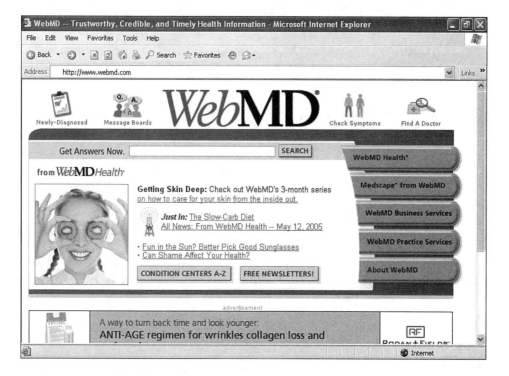

FIGURE 8.1

At WebMD you can check your symptoms, find a doctor, or interact with others on the message boards.

MayoClinic.com (www.mayoclinic.com) is a reputable website that provides many tools for helping people live healthier lives. There is information on first aid, food, and nutrition, as well as tools and techniques to help you monitor your health. Don't overlook this site if you are searching for information on specific diseases and conditions. It covers everything from asthma to mental health.

Our wonderful colleges and universities are also great resources when searching for health information. The Virtual Hospital (www.vh.org) is an excellent digital library of medical information from the University of Iowa. The Oregon Health & Science University's consumer health resources can be found by clicking on the Consumer Health link at the OHSU library website at www.ohsu.edu/library.

Here are a few more informative medical websites for you to check out:

✓ Medscape, an offshoot of WebMD, provides specialty home pages for specific categories such as urology, cardiology, and infectious diseases (www.medscape.com) .

✓ The Internet Public Library has a ton of health and medical information. Just click on the Health link at www.ipl.org.

✓ A comprehensive health and medicine library can be found at www.digital-librarian.com/health.html.

✓ The Yahoo! Health Directory categorizes many health resources. It can be found at http://dir.yahoo.com/Health/Medicine.

✓ The Health and Medicine Facts Encyclopedia from Refdesk.com (www.refdesk.com/health.html) gives information on everything from anthrax to urology.

✓ Med Help International's "Virtual Medical Center for Patients" (www.medhelp.org) is a collection of information and professional medical support gathered from medical organizations and experts around the world.

Trivia

Improvements in health care have allowed people to live longer. In 1900 there were 100,000 Americans over the age of 85. In 2000, 4.2 million had already celebrated their eighty-fifth birthday.

Health Information for Boomers and Beyond

The government might be the last place you would expect to find good health information. If so, the U. S. Administration on Aging website (www.aoa.dhhs.gov) might surprise you. It has a wealth of information on aging including Medicare and disability information. They even have information on several initiatives that encourage Americans to make healthier choices.

You can find more health information for people as they move toward their boomer and zoomer years at Health and Age (www.healthandage.com). This website has health centers for Alzheimer's, diabetes, hearing, vision, memory, and many other health-related topics (see Figure 8.2).

FIGURE 8.2
"Live Well, Live Longer" is the motto of the Health and Age website.

The National Institute of Health's SeniorHealth.gov website at http://nihseniorhealth.gov also has good solid medical information. At this website you can learn about macular degeneration, balance problems, low vision, shingles, and more.

Becoming a Discerning Information Seeker

Anyone can state her opinion on the Internet. Unfortunately, sometimes it's hard to tell the difference between opinion and fact. It is extremely important to remember this when you are looking for health information. Although there are many reputable organizations with websites, there are also websites with misinformation. You need to be discerning when visiting any medical website. If the site sells health care products, be sure it is not making positive statements only to help sell its wares.

BLOOPER ALERT

Being skeptical is healthy. Remember, not all the information found on the Internet is accurate. Check the reputation of the source of the information before taking it as fact.

Always check out who is behind the website. You can do this by looking around the website, finding contact information, and reading any privacy statements or other website data. Some medical sites are solely Web-based. These sites require a little more scrutiny than websites that are affiliated with well-known medical institutions or universities.

There are several "watchdog" groups that can help you decide if information is based on scientific studies or opinion. These groups evaluate websites based on standards they have set. If the website meets their criteria, they are allowed to display the symbol of that group. Some of these groups are

- URAC (http://webapps.urac.org)
- HONcode; Health on the Net Foundation Code of Conduct (www.hon.ch/HONcode/Conduct.html)
- TRUSTe, a privacy statement (www.truste.org)

Learning the Medical Lingo

Like it or not, you are often thrown into the complex world of medical terminology. Doctors blurt out words like colonoscopy, carcinoma, or angioplasty. They often don't take the time to explain these terms to the patient. If you find you need a detailed explanation on any medical term, the Internet will come to your aid.

The MedlinePlus website at http://medlineplus.gov has an excellent medical encyclopedia and dictionary to help you understand all that medical lingo. This website is a service of the U.S. National Library of Medicine and the National Institutes of Health. It is another government-sponsored website that is filled with useful health information. It even has videos of surgical procedures—a little bloody, but often useful and informative.

To find more valuable explanations of medical terminology, surf over to MedicineNet.com (www.medicinenet.com), see Figure 8.3. Click on the MedTerms Dictionary tab to look up any of those unfamiliar medical terms. The Procedures & Tests tab will give you information on medical tests from bone density scans to coronary balloon angioplasty.

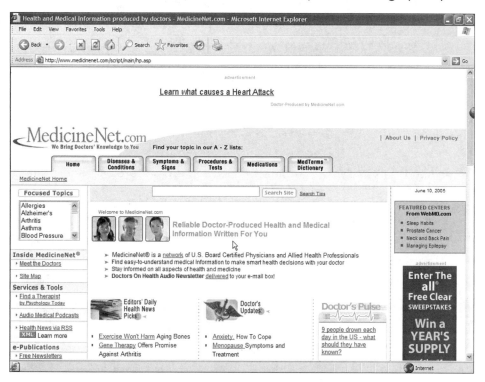

FIGURE 8.3

At the MedicineNet.com website you can look up medical terms by entering them in a search box or choosing a letter of the alphabet.

Martindale's Virtual Medical Center at www.martindalecenter.com/Medical.html has links to medical dictionaries. It also has thousands of tutorials and links to other valuable resources.

Finding Support Groups Online

In the "good old days," you might never meet another individual who had the same disease or condition. Today, no matter how rare your affliction, the Internet can help you find others who have similar conditions. You can learn about their experiences, ask them questions, and share knowledge about drugs and treatments. The number of online support groups is constantly growing.

The benefits to individuals and their families are immeasurable. Those who live in isolated locations no longer have to do without a support group because they don't live near one. Those who are unable to get out can venture online for help. Even if they already belong to a local group, they can get additional help from these online support groups.

Many find being able to access an online support group, such as the Breast Cancer Support site shown in Figure 8.4, during a serious illness is like being tossed a lifeline in their time of need.

Make sure the support group or groups you are considering are valid, and are, in fact, only there to benefit their members. If they ask for money, financial information, or other personal information before you can join, you need to be extremely careful. A good support group will be there to meet *your* needs, and will not ask you to meet theirs.

BLOOPER ALERT

Be careful when sharing information in a support group. Even though you might feel a personal connection, you always need to guard your private information.

A good place to start looking for a support group is at Google's directory of support groups. The Web address is http://directory.google.com/Top/Society/Support_Groups. Google provides subcategories to choose from, as well as listings in the main category. When you investigate, you will find an amazing number of groups in every kind of category imaginable. For instance, click the Health category and then click Conditions and Diseases, and you will find more than 19,000 listings.

FIGURE 8.4
The Breast Cancer Support site at www.bcsupport.org was created to support breast cancer survivors.

Although one of the most popular sites to find support groups, Google is by no means the only place to look. Other options you might try include

- The Virtual Wellness Community at www.thewellnesscommunity.org was created to help people with all types of cancer (see Figure 8.5).

- SupportWorks at www.supportworks.org will help you find a support group in your local area or one on the Web.

- SupportPath at www.supportpath.com has an online support group chat. It also gives information on national events.

- Genetic and Rare Conditions Site at www.kumc.edu/gec/support has information on support groups, as well as facts on genetic and rare diseases.

- The Healing Exchange Brain Trust at www.braintrust.org has special interest online email groups for various brain-related disorders.

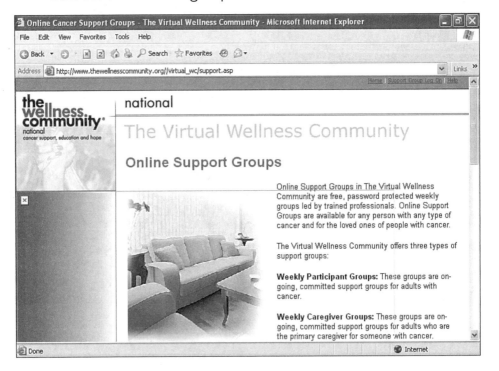

FIGURE 8.5
The online support groups at the Virtual Wellness Community have many different types of support for cancer victims.

Another simple way to find support groups is to use a search engine to enter the name of the disease or condition. This will, without a doubt, give you links that will lead to support groups.

For more information on search engines, see Chapter 2, "Search and Learn Online."

High-Tech Health Solutions

Technology is making a huge impact on everything related to health and wellness. Improvements in medical testing, advances in medical equipment, and breakthroughs in medication are improving the health of millions. This is one place that we will all offer a big hurrah for technology since it is helping us live longer and more comfortable lives.

Resources for Healthy Vision

When it comes to our vision, the advances in medical technology are almost unbelievable. Today, we can have cataracts removed and we can use laser surgery to make near-sighted or far-sighted vision almost perfect. Most of us now take LASIK surgery for granted.

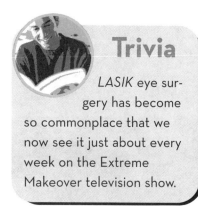

Trivia

LASIK eye surgery has become so commonplace that we now see it just about every week on the Extreme Makeover television show.

If you have a vision problem, you are not alone. There are an estimated 37 million blind people in the world and another 124 million people who suffer from low vision.

It will take years for the technological breakthroughs that are now occurring to help all of these people, but it is comforting to know that technology is making progress. High-tech magnifiers and other devices are great aids to those with vision problems. The JORDY glasses, a system of camera and head-worn glasses by Enhanced Vision (www.enhancedvision.com) is now helping some who are legally blind to see again (see Figure 8.6).

There are also many online resources for vision information. You can visit these sites to find information about treatments, technology aids, and procedures that would be best for your particular set of circumstances. If you have macular degeneration, glaucoma, or other eye problems, you can find detailed information by simply entering the disease or condition into any search engine. Be sure to visit the general medical websites mentioned earlier in this chapter—many have entire areas dedicated to vision.

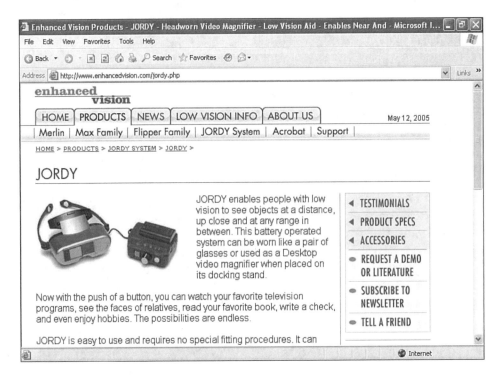

FIGURE 8.6
The JORDY glasses by Enhanced Vision have allowed some legally blind people to see again.

Some other vision sites you might want to investigate include

- International Centre for Eye Health (www.iceh.org.uk)

- Healthy Vision 2010 (www.healthyvision2010.org)

- Healthy Living—Healthy Vision (www.preventblindness.org/ healthy_living)

- Links to resources and web pages (http://directory.google.com/Top/Health/Senses/Vision)

Help for the Hearing Impaired

Did you know that Bill Clinton, Arnold Palmer, and William Shatner all wear hearing aides? Barbara Streisand, David Letterman, Peter Jennings, and Steve Martin also have hearing loss.

Hearing loss is something that often occurs gradually, without the immediate knowledge of the person suffering from it. Often, those trying to communicate with them notice it first, when they need to repeat what they've said, or what they have said is frequently misunderstood. Science has yet to find a way to actually restore hearing, but many advances have been made in this field.

Profoundly deaf individuals, for example, can have partial hearing restored through the use of electrical stimulation or cochlear implants. However, for the rest of us, hearing aids are the best option. Although hearing cannot, at this point, be completely restored, dramatic technological advances have been made in hearing aid technology. Effectiveness, size reduction, and attractiveness have all seen great improvements. Although you might have seen Bill Clinton and William Shatner on television numerous times, you might not have realized that they wear hearing aids. The hearing aids are so small that they can hardly be seen.

When looking for hearing aids, remember not to expect perfection. They don't give you perfect hearing like reading glasses can give you perfect vision, although medical technologies give us reason to hope for this in the future.

Hearing aids come in two main varieties: analog (the older type) and the newer digital versions. Most experts agree that the analog variety will soon be phased out and only digital ones will be used. Prices for hearing aids can run from $100

Trivia

Baby boomers suffer from a higher degree of hearing loss than any generation before them. Of the 75 million Americans born between 1945 and 1964, 16 million (more than 20%) have some degree of hearing loss.

Sandy's tip

Excessive noise is the number one reason for hearing loss. Boom boxes, loud entertainment systems, power tools, motorcycles, and other loud equipment all contribute to hearing loss. So tone it down, and make sure the kids and grandkids do, too.

all the way to $2,200. Some of the higher-end aids work with voice-activation technology. Others can be programmed and adjusted by putting them in a computer to change settings that, in turn, provide the appropriate level of hearing.

Although most of us would prefer to have small, unobtrusive hearing aids, smaller is not necessarily better for all individuals. Many sufferers of hearing loss also have other health problems, such as arthritis, shaky hands, or loss of visual acuity. This can be problematic when dealing with very small hearing devices. Because hearing aids need to be inserted and removed for cleaning and battery replacement, some will be better off with larger hearing aids.

Trivia

The ear has more than 25,000 tiny hair cells to help you hear different sounds.

Improvements provided by hearing aids can be profound. When wearing their hearing aids for the first few days or weeks, individuals will often comment that they hadn't realized how much they were missing. They can go to family outings and hear all the conversations, or go to a symphony and fully enjoy it. The change in lifestyle can be dramatic and very rewarding.

There are many websites that have information on hearing loss. The Hear-It website at www.hear-it.org has facts and figures on hearing loss as well as links to related news articles and information on how hearing loss affects our lifestyle (see Figure 8.7). The Better Hearing Institute at www.betterhearing.org has interesting articles on hearing loss, solutions, and prevention.

Oral Health

Recent research has attributed certain illnesses (such as heart disease) to poor dental health. Great strides are being made in the dental field to encourage the general public to improve dental health. One way of doing that is to make procedures less painful.

FIGURE 8.7
The Hear-It website has interesting information on hearing loss.

Advances in laser technology are making this possible. For example, dental implants are now being done with little to no pain. Using a laser instead of a scalpel, there's no cutting and no blood. There's no need for Novocain. Patients can return to their normal lives with very little soreness immediately after the implant is done.

Lasers are also being used for the treatment of cavities, receding gums, and other dental problems. One of the benefits of this type of treatment is much improved healing time. The biggest benefit, say dentists, is that patients no longer

BLOOPER ALERT
Be sure to check with your insurance carrier to see if a new type of procedure is covered before having it performed. Some laser procedures are covered by insurance, but it pays to check ahead of time.

dread visits to the dentist. They can make routine dental checkups as ordinary as running everyday errands.

For more information on laser dentistry, visit Laser Dentistry in America at www.laserdentistryinamerica.com.

Digital Devices and Resources for Healthier Living

There have been many developments in high-tech devices in recent years. As a result, the way we live continues to change at an amazing pace. Even the little things have changed. You probably remember how painful it was to remove a Band-Aid when you were a kid. Today we have "ouch-less" Band-Aids. We have hot and cold packs that can be activated without any heating or cooling. We have also gone well beyond these small improvements. Today we have improved medical tests, newly-found medications, and wonderful high-tech devices like blood pressure and blood sugar monitors that give "instant" results.

Using Digital Resources to Stay Healthy

Today, even without a degree in medicine, you can use a digital blood pressure monitor to check your blood pressure at home. Home kits are available to test the sugar or cholesterol level in your blood. Many of the tasks that previously could only be accomplished in a doctor's office can now be done at home or when traveling. As a result, we can monitor our health to prevent disease, rather than wait until the disease has attacked.

Sandy's tip
Remember, health and fitness can make the difference between living well and just living.

Digital devices have become so commonplace that we often take them for granted. For instance, do you remember the last time your physician or hospital used a thermometer that wasn't digital? Even the old way of taking your blood pressure using a pump action sphygmomanometer is being phased out in favor of the new digital blood pressure monitors.

There are plenty of high-tech devices to keep you healthy. A pedometer will keep track of how far you walk, hopefully encouraging you to keep on moving. New bathroom scales can give you your weight, tell you how many pounds you need to lose to reach your goal, and check your body mass index. You can use a wristwatch-like blood pressure monitor to keep track of your heart rate while you exercise. A company named Coolibar (www.coolibar.com) makes sun protective clothing you can wear to prevent those harmful rays of the sun from damaging your skin.

Electronic Medical Records

Electronic medical records (EMR) is a generic term used to describe computer-based patient medical records. The term has been expanded to include systems that keep track of other relevant medical information. EMRs help clinical staff look up patient data more easily, accurately complete insurance claims processing, and automatically check for drug and allergy interactions.

With the use of EMRs comes the inevitable question of privacy and security. Although security breaches are a possibility, medical records can remain as secure as your bank account information if the proper protocols are followed. To this end, the Health Insurance Portability and Accountability Act of 1996, Public Law 104-191 (HIPAA), also known as the "Kennedy-Kassebaum Act," was introduced. This law provides standards for patient health, administrative, and financial data interchange. In other words, it governs the privacy and security of health information records and transactions. This law took effect in 2001. Full compliance was required by 2004. If you would like more information on HIPAA, you can visit the website at www.cms.hhs.gov/hipaa.

LINGO

HIPAA, Title II is the Health Insurance Portability and Accountability Act of 1996 that governs the privacy and security of health information records and transactions.

Sandy's tip
Medical experts tell us the sooner diagnosis can be made, the better the success rate for beating cancer.

Digital Imaging

At last! Ladies, there is now technology available to get a digital mammography! It's called *"full-field digital mammography."* Does this eliminate the way we have experienced mammographies in the past? Not quite. However, GE's full-field digital mammography takes excellent images of breast tissue in about half the time needed for the traditional film-based mammograms. The exceptional detail and sharpness provided allow health care providers to diagnose small cancers sooner and more accurately than ever before.

With this type of mammogram, the total amount of time needed for a mammography appointment can now be brought down to about 20 minutes. Another positive factor of digital images is that scans are captured, read, stored, and can be transferred to the physician in digital format. Therefore, they can be read more quickly and easily, even if the health care provider is in a location which is remote from the testing center. For more information on digital mammograms, visit herSource.com at www.hersource.com.

LINGO

Magnetic resonance imaging (MRI) uses a powerful magnetic field and radio waves to alter the natural alignment of hydrogen atoms within the body. Computers are used to record the activity of the hydrogen atoms and translate that into images.

When this same type of technology is used in magnetic resonance imaging (MRI), the same sort of advantages is exhibited. The digital technology means higher resolution images. Less time needed for the imaging process means greater comfort for the patient.

A computed axial tomography scan (CT or CAT), gives the diagnostician a way of looking inside the human body. The images produced are cross-sectional, sometimes compared to slices in a loaf of bread. During this exam the scanner takes multiple cross-sectional images. A computer helps create these images and the images are capable of depicting various internal body parts in great detail, enhancing the physician's ability to diagnose a variety of medical conditions, including cancer and heart disease.

LINGO

A *computer axial tomography scan* (CT or *CAT)* is the process of using digital processing to generate a three-dimensional image of the internals of a patient using a series of two-dimensional X-ray images taken around a single axis of rotation.

The Technology of the Future Is Here Now

Medical technology is moving quickly, finding cures for disease, creating equipment to help the disabled, and developing new techniques for medical testing. There is great hope for the future, but even today we can do things we never even dreamed of. Monkeys have been able to move a cursor on a computer screen using only the power of their thoughts. The iBOT wheelchair can travel up and down stairs and across grass and sand. The JORDY glasses help those who are nearly blind to see. We haven't yet reached the medical know-how of the Star Trek Enterprise, but we are moving quickly in that direction.

Personal BioChips

Personalized biochips are already being used for medical and security purposes. Both implanted chips and portable devices are available for medical records. It is estimated that by 2015, nearly everyone will carry their health and medical records with them, either in some sort of jewelry or as an implanted chip that will be easily read and understood. These chips or devices will contain vital statistics, blood type, allergies, and even your individual DNA to help identify people and their medical needs. In the future, these biochips may even be used for granting access to cars, homes, or computers (not unlike the voice recognitions and retinal scan devices of today).

Virtual Medicine

Monitors in intensive care units have been computerized for some time. Usually, a nurse is in a room where the monitors of several patients can be seen at once. New technology is carrying this idea further. A doctor can now monitor several patients at different facilities from a central location. Monitors display vital signs. Video screens, microphones, and speakers allow the doctor to observe each patient and evaluate his condition. The doctor has a webcam and microphone as well, so that if the patient can see the doctor on a screen in his room, they can converse in "real time."

The ramifications of this technology are limitless. A doctor in another city or even a different country can "see" the patient and provide consultation. In remote areas, doctors can walk trained medical personnel through simple procedures. Specialists can "consult" via cameras in surgery and "assist" the surgeons onsite in performing surgical procedures. This will result in better care with less travel for both the patient and the health care professional. Hopefully, it will also translate into lower health care costs.

Some predict that in the future many doctor's visits will be "virtual visits." You won't have to leave home to consult with your doctor. In-home technology will allow the doctor to examine you and make a diagnosis. When this happens, we will have come full circle. Although they will only be virtual visits, doctors will be making house calls once again!

In the near future, circulatory, heart, or kidney testing might be as easy as a home pregnancy test. After you have administered one or more of these tests to yourself or a family member, you will be able to transmit the results to your doctor over the Internet. The doctor will then respond by telling you what to do, or by sending other health care professionals to your home to administer additional tests. You will be able to converse with your doctor "face-to-face" via webcams and computers and discuss possible options for treatment.

If you don't think that this will ever happen, you'd better think again. Insurance companies that have a vested interest in keeping health costs down are actively pursuing and promoting these technologies. Schools and research labs are bringing these technologies closer and closer every day.

Advances in Surgical Procedures

The future of some surgeries and medical procedures might be in wireless technology. One example is the capsule endoscopy. This procedure uses a tiny capsule with a camera inside. The patient swallows the capsule, which then works a little like the Hubble Telescope to look inside the intestines. While passing through the digestive tract, the camera wirelessly transmits images of the intestine to a receiver that is worn around the patient's waist. These images are then downloaded to a computer where they can be examined by a physician. Devices like this might eliminate the need for standard endoscopies and other uncomfortable procedures in the future.

Sandy's Summary

In just a few short years the Internet has revolutionized health care. It has put the resources we need to take charge of our own health at our fingertips. We can research symptoms, diseases, medicine, and cures. We can learn about the latest health initiatives. And we can use this information to improve our health and to implement a healthier lifestyle.

Armed with more and better information, we can ask the right questions when we visit the doctor. After our visit we can get an explanation of the medical lingo that was thrown at us with a simple trip to the Internet.

We must learn to be discerning when dealing with health issues on the Web. It is also advisable to find out who is behind a website and where their medical information comes from.

Support groups abound on the Internet. These are valuable resources for many diseases and disorders. They can lend support and personal interaction to help us make it through medical problems.

Technology has made it easier to maintain health and fitness with devices such as blood pressure monitors. Laser dentistry, eye surgery, digital hearing aids, and MRIs—all show how technology is improving the quality of our lives.

As we move even deeper into the digital age, electronic medical records will help us track medications, allergies, and health conditions. Pharmacists, physicians, and other health care providers will use these records to give us better care. As virtual medicine catches on, the days of doctor's house calls may even reappear, virtually.

There's no doubt about it, the Internet and technology has increased our life spans and given us healthier bodies with which to enjoy our extra time here on earth. Improved research and development in the medical field is sure to supply even more benefits in the near future. It's exciting to be a part of it all!

Sandy Berger

Chapter 9

Meeting People Online

"Every man can tell how many goats or sheep he possesses, but not how many friends."

—Marcus Tullius Cicero

I've often said that the Internet mirrors the real world and this certainly holds true when we talk of community life. We are physically a part of a local community, where we can join clubs, churches, and neighbor groups. On the Web, we are a part of the Internet community where the variety of groups is even larger.

It's human nature to gather to share common interests. So it's not surprising that Internet communities have sprung up spontaneously. Millions worldwide have discovered that Internet communities can offer them the camaraderie and support they seek. It's just like being with a group of friends but instead of being down the street, at church, or in the neighborhood bar, your friends are waiting for

In This Chapter

- Internet Communities
- Online Friendships and Dating
- Child Safety Online

you online. Rather than just surfing the web, being a part of Internet communities is actually like colonizing cyberspace.

Internet Communities

More and more people going online today return to the same sites repeatedly instead of searching for new sites. A vast majority consider themselves part of an online community. What this really shows us is that, as in normal life, we like to congregate, and the Internet, as has been done before, is being molded to meet our needs. If you're thinking we're mainly talking about young people, you're wrong; young, old, or somewhere in between, we're all finding our comfort zones on the Internet.

How do you define a web community? They are as different as the many people that come together to enjoy them. Although there are some general communities, it is more common to find groups that are based on a common interest. There are communities that center around work-related activities, as well. Whatever your vocation (or avocation), you can find a community with that focus. A really good community also encourages interaction and communication among its members. There might be a structure and a set of guidelines, or the website might be completely available to be molded by the members. These are truly virtual communities.

Types of Communities

There are several types of web communities. Some websites have message boards where visitors can interact with each other. Some have chat rooms. Some have both.

Message Boards

On a message board, which is sometimes called a *forum*, you post your message and it appears on the message board for comment by anyone who happens to be visiting at that moment or in the future. You can look at your message at anytime and read the responses. Some message boards allow you to post anonymously without signing up for the board. Most message boards, however, require that you sign in and get a username and password to post messages. Having a username and password is valuable because then everyone recognizes your username and gets to know who you are by reading your posts. This encourages the sense of community and makes visiting message boards more fun.

Chat Rooms

Chat rooms are different in that they are time-related. A chat room is live. You can gather in a chat room to have a discussion with a pre-announced expert or celebrity. You can also visit an open chat room at any time to converse with others who happen to be there at that time. It is really like chatting at the neighborhood bar, outside of church, or when you meet people on the street corner because it occurs in real time (unlike email or message boards) and can be a back-and-forth banter through typed messages.

LINGO

Chatting on the Internet involves going to an address on the Internet that two or more people can visit at once to interact with each other by typing messages back and forth in real time.

Internet Discussion Groups

Internet discussion groups are similar to message boards where you can post messages and read everyone's messages and responses. Discussion groups, like message boards, can be very helpful to visitors, often giving an answer to an important question and sometimes providing a much needed idea that turns a light bulb on in the visitor's head. Most discussion groups have email capabilities. You can be emailed every post, a daily digest of posts, or no email at all. Often discussion groups are not as community-like as message boards. Message boards tend to attract more users who become involved in more personal posts. Discussion groups, for the most part, are not as personal. Many

Blooper Alert

Be aware that if you choose to be emailed every post for an active discussion group, your inbox can quickly fill up with email from the discussion group.

discussion groups, however, also allow you to set up your own mailing list and have a private group.

What a Community Site Offers You

Today's cyber citizens gather in groups for many reasons. Many need camaraderie and companionship. Some venture online during a lonely time in their lives.

They might be seeking advice or a support group when they first go online. Although they probably will find what they are after, they also find something more lasting and fulfilling—a community of people who share similar experiences, people who understand.

Becoming a part of an Internet community can be a welcome experience or a life-changing event, depending upon the individual's needs and the community (or communities) they discover. Many say they can't believe the changes that have occurred in their lives as a result. And we're not talking about just a few hundred people. Instead of only going online to surf various sites and get bits of information or buy those necessary items, this new set of Internet Citizens (Netizens for short) are finding a community they like, settling in, and finding a new "home away from home" for themselves. They still seek information and use the Internet for all the reasons they used to, but they have discovered a new sense of community online. There is a sense of being welcome in this group of friends. It has been compared to walking into a neighborhood bar, like on the TV series *Cheers*, where everyone knows you and is glad to see you.

Some people find their first experiences online a little overwhelming. There's just so much stuff out there that it's a little hard to comprehend. That's all the more reason to find that comfortable place to visit and to return to it on a regular basis.

Finding a Community That Understands You

Like pen pals of old, the Internet makes it easy for people from around the world to meet and become friends. Meeting people is easy. Start at places that interest you. Then look for message boards and chat rooms where you can converse with others about your hobbies and interests.

Some of the biggest names in the Internet have created Internet communities. AOL has many communities in its AOL People Connection (http://pc.channel.aol.com), as shown in Figure 9.1. At AOL you can find an old-fashioned pen pal, with the high-tech twist that everything is done online. No one is left out at AOL. Other areas in its People Connection include Friends & Flirts, Gay & Lesbian, and AOL Pets. AOL has special chat rooms and content that is available only for members, but the AOL People Connection is open to all.

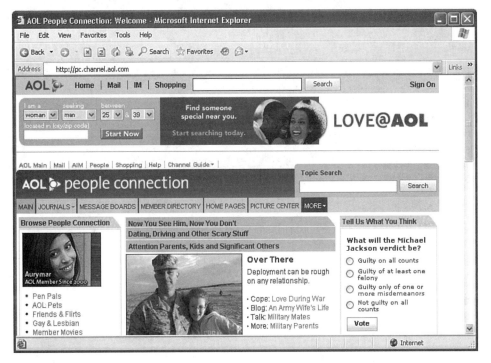

FIGURE 9.1
The AOL People Connection has many options for meeting people.

You can also find a community website geared to your age and sex.

AARP at www.aarp.org is one site that focuses its content on the over-50 crowd. It has articles on many issues and provides community message boards for various topics, as shown in Figure 9.2. At AARP you can find message boards on health and wellness, money and work, travel, fun and games, and of course my favorite, learning and technology. The AARP technology message board has many regulars who ask and answer questions and interact with each other. You don't have to be a member to access the AARP website and you don't have to feel like a "senior." They have plenty of vibrant information, especially in the Computers and Technology, Travel, and Health areas.

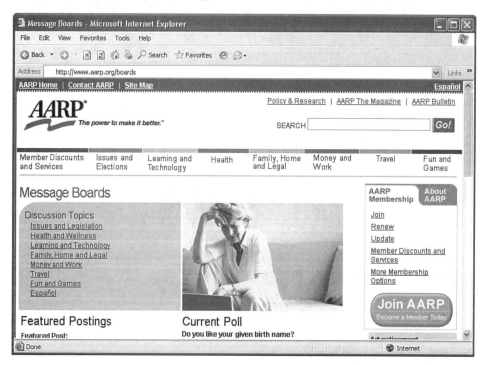

FIGURE 9.2
The AARP website has a good variety of special interest message boards.

Women of all ages are drawn to the female-oriented content at the iVillage website at www.ivillage.com. Its Message Board Central area, shown in Figure 9.3, has choices ranging from Beauty & Style to Country Living.

Another great way to find community-type websites is to visit websites geared to your interests and then look for message boards and chat rooms. You are sure to find them when you put your antenna out. For instance, if you are a movie fan, look into message boards and chats at movie-related websites. You will quickly find that one of the biggest movie websites, IMDb, has message boards at www.imdb.com/boards. The DVD Review website at www.dvdreview.com has discussion topics on everything from horror and cult films to hardware and home theater equipment. You can also get others' opinions on the best and worst movies to see.

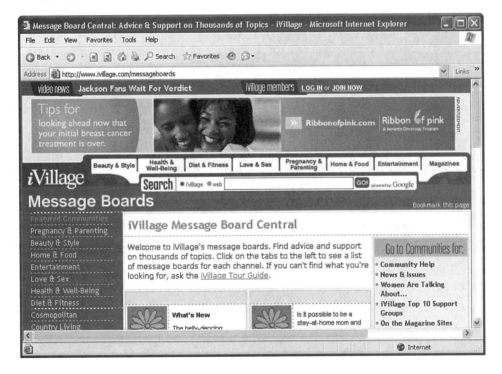

FIGURE 9.3
iVillage specializes in message boards with a feminine flair.

Health is another topic where you can find plenty of spirited community message boards. Use any search engine to find health-related websites. These message boards are generally geared toward a specific health topic or disease. For instance you can easily find message boards related to Alzheimer's, cancer, and dieting. If you are looking for health message boards, check out HealthBoards.com at www.healthboards.com. It has more than 120 boards covering topics ranging from acne to women's health. Diseases such as immune disorders, infectious diseases, and many others are covered. There are even boards that discuss Viagra, menopause, and smoking cessation.

The MedHelp Q & A Medical and Health Forums at www.medhelp.org/forums.htm is a great place to find patient-to-patient support message boards on topics such as nutrition, weight loss, dental health, and eye care. They also have question-and-answer message boards on arthritis, breast cancer, diabetes, and many other health-related topics.

Although Internet discussion groups are usually less community-oriented, they are still a great place to get information and strike up a conversation. These groups are more like being in a large group of people and being able to eavesdrop on all the conversations and add you own comments and questions whenever you like. One of the best places to find Internet discussion groups is at Google Groups at http://groups-beta.google.com, as shown in Figure 9.4. Another popular group consolidator is Yahoo!. You can find its group section at http://groups.yahoo.com. At either of these sites you can join a group with common interests. There are thousands to choose from including business, finance, computers, culture, education, games, music, and romance. All of these are free (supported by ads) and are well worth a look. Yahoo! also has a complete listing of message boards at http://messages.yahoo.com/index.html. Current events, hobbies, fitness, stocks, genealogy, cyberculture, and food and drink are just a few of the many topics covered.

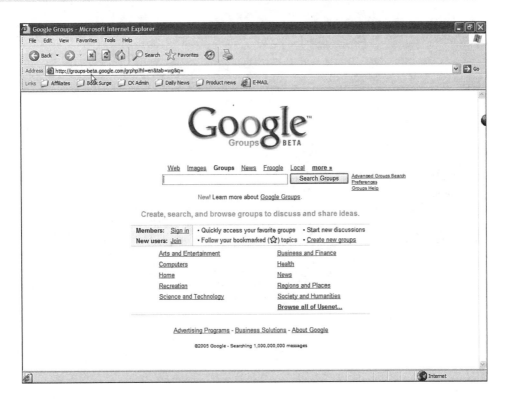

FIGURE 9.4
Google Groups has an excellent variety of groups on just about every topic imaginable.

Chat rooms can be found at many community websites. If you love to chat, try Talk City (www.talkcity.com) as shown in Figure 9.5. Talk City charges for special membership privileges, but access to its 200+ chat rooms is free with registration. It has chat rooms including desperate housewives, 40s plus, sports, Christian singles, and plenty of adult chats.

FIGURE 9.5
Talk City is a good place to look for chat rooms.

No matter what your hobbies or interests, there are sure to be others on the Web who share your enthusiasm. Find your own community and settle in.

Online Friendship and Dating

Do you start feeling lonely when family oriented holidays approach? No mate? Not a soul to talk to? No valentines coming your way? Don't feel bad. You're not alone. An October 2003 Nielsen//NetRatings report found that the online friend and dating community was one of the most popular social networks on the Web. It attracted almost a million visitors in October 2003, and you can bet the numbers have climbed since then. Why not? The Internet is a great place to meet and communicate with others.

For safety's sake, be sure that you never give out your real name or any personal information in a message board, chat room, or dating website. It is a good idea to get a different email address to use only on such sites. In many cases your Internet provider will gladly add an extra email name to your account. Or you can use Hotmail (www.hotmail.com) to get a new email address specifically for this purpose. Be sure to use a moniker rather than your real name for this account.

Check out CyberAngels at www.cyberangels.org, shown in Figure 9.6, for more information about chat room and online safety. (See more about safety in the next section of this chapter.)

FIGURE 9.6
CyberAngels is the world's oldest and largest Internet safely organization.

Just Looking for a Friend?

Just looking for some companionship rather than a serious relationship? Several websites accommodate e-dating as well as friendly encounters.

At Friendster (www.friendster.com) you can find old classmates, share photos with friends, and even create a friendly blog. You can also join public groups, participate in discussions, and create private groups. Friendster currently boasts more than 17 million members.

Meetup, shown in Figure 9.7, is another popular social networking site. This takes a slightly different slant. Meetup helps you find people who share your interests and live in your own physical community. You can search Meetup by interest or by location. Meetup Groups meet monthly in a community area. They are informal and are open to anyone. Therefore, you can bring along a friend or two to check out the group on your first few meetings. There are Meetup Groups focused on many different topics. You might find one related to a health condition and another working for a political candidate. There are Meetup Groups all over the United States and in more than 40 different countries.

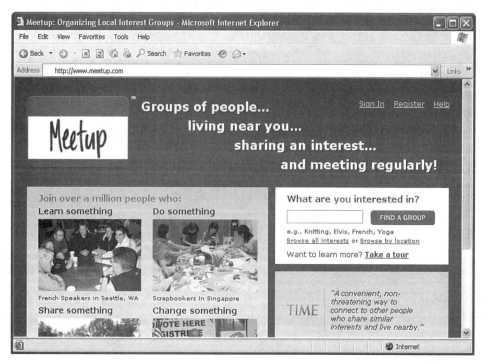

FIGURE 9.7

The Meetup website provides a way for you to find local groups in your community for face-to-face group meetings.

Google has also joined the online social networks with the launch of Orkut (www.orkut.com), which is an invitation-only friend site. (You must be invited to join by a current member.)

Dating

Anyone who has watched the movie *You've Got Mail* might be interested in a successful Internet relationship that turns into a real-life romance. There are plenty of websites that will help you find Mr. or Mrs. Right.

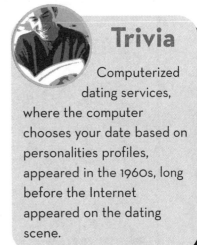

Trivia

Computerized dating services, where the computer chooses your date based on personalities profiles, appeared in the 1960s, long before the Internet appeared on the dating scene.

Online romance sites have become extremely popular. I'll bet you're asking yourself if these websites really work. Well, it's like meeting someone in real life. Sometimes they work and sometimes they don't. I will tell you that I have heard from people who have had all kinds of experiences with online dating sites. Most, it seems, will find compatible mates, but only time and experience can reveal the true personality of a person. One friend of mine moved to a different state to be with a "fantastic, wonderfully compatible" man she met on the Internet. After a year she moved back to her home state after being bilked out of several thousand dollars. On the other hand, a friend who is a highly successful lawyer met her dream man on the Internet, and after several years, they are poised to live happily ever after.

Most online dating websites charge a fee for their services. You fill out an extensive questionnaire and are then paired with potentially compatible people. Some will allow you to fill out the questionnaire and give you pairings for free. They then charge you a monthly membership fee to access their websites where you can communicate with and get to know your potential mate.

Here are a few of the most popular dating websites:

- Date.com, which is found at (you guessed it!) www.date.com

- eHarmony at www.eharmony.com (shown in Figure 9.8)

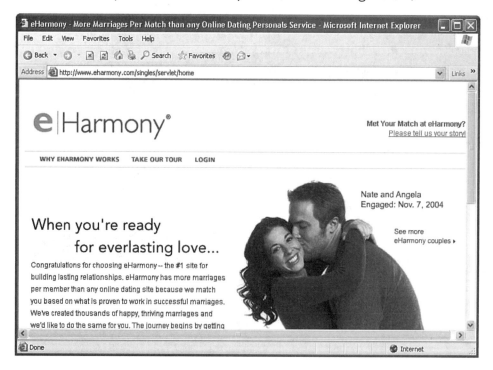

FIGURE 9.8
eHarmony helps you find a date or even a mate.

- Match.com at www.match.com (of course!)

- Matchmaker at www.matchmaker.com

- TheSpark at http://community.sparknotes.com

- udate at www.udate.com

You might also try dating websites that help you find just the kind of person you are looking for. For example, jdate at www.jdate.com is the largest network of Jewish singles on the Web. Special meeting places such as Gay.com at www.gay.com help gay individuals find their own special mates.

If you are a boomer and are looking for someone your age, you can meet other boomers at the BABYBOOMERPeopleMeet website (www.babyboomerpeoplemeet.com), as shown in Figure 9.9. I got a kick out of a website called SeniorFriendFinder.com (www. seniorfriendfinder.com). This site states that it is for "dating for people with experience." The member search allows you to search for members from 25 to 99. It used to be that you were called a senior after 65, then that moved to 55, and then to 50. At this website I guess even twenty-five-year-olds are feeling those senior moments. In any case, this site says it is a popular place for people over 40 looking to meet others for romance, dating, friendship, and more.

FIGURE 9.9
The BABYBOOMERPeopleMeet website specializes in bringing together people from 40 to 59 years old.

If you are new to the cyber-singles scene, you might want to check out the personals section of your Internet service provider. Many large

Internet providers, such as AOL and EarthLink, provide areas where members can get to know each other.

It can be difficult to decide which dating website you might like to try. Most of these sites, such as Matchmaker (shown in Figure 9.10), allow you to take a tour of the website, which will give you a good idea of how their process works.

FIGURE 9.10
The Matchmaker website lets you flirt with others or get serious.

Whatever you do, don't feel that you are alone. Many people are looking for their soul mates. The udate website says that more than 5,000 people join udate everyday.

Whether you are looking for someone to talk to or someone to love, there is no doubt that the Internet can be one of the ways for you to meet people. By the way, when Jupiter Research recently examined online dating activities by gender, they found that men looking for love on the Internet outnumbered women by quite a margin. So go girls!

Sandy's tip
Some dating sites give you a free personality profile and some free time to try out their services. Shop around; offers vary.

Cautious Cyber Relations

Whether you meet someone in a chat room or through an online dating service, the first rule of thumb is to take it slowly. You might think that you know the person because you have been chatting or corresponding via email, but remember to use common sense. Here are a few extra things you can do to keep yourself safe.

Use Extra-Safe Dating Sites

Most dating websites begin by asking you to fill out a profile. Before you do, make sure you read the privacy policy of the website. I often think of a poster that I saw several years ago about the anonymity of the Internet. It was a large picture of a German shepherd with a caption that read, "On the Internet no one knows I'm a dog." Many people who visit Internet dating sites are not completely honest. Although I advise you to be honest, please realize that others might stretch the truth a little (or a lot). In a recent Nielsen//NetRatings' analysis of the online dating community, out of those acknowledging they accessed an online dating service the previous day, 11% were married individuals. And those were the ones being honest!

Websites have sprung up that actually try to keep people honest. A website called MyCountryMatch at www.mycountrymatch.com makes everyone pledge that they are single and unattached as well as honest and truthful. Another website called True, at www.true.com/default.htm, has teamed up with Rapsheets Criminal Records to do background checks on each person it matches up, as shown in Figure 9.11. With all of this, keep in mind that no web service is perfect. Your future mate might be somewhere on the Internet, but go slowly, use common sense, and always be at least a little suspicious.

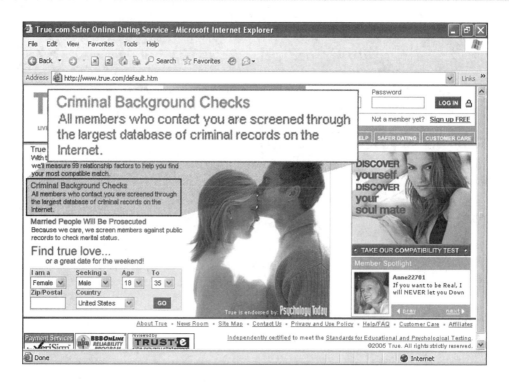

FIGURE 9.11
The True online dating service screens members with criminal background checks.

Guard Your Anonymity

Be sure *not* to include your last name, address, workplace, phone number, or any other identifying information when corresponding online. Most online dating services use a double-blind system that protects your identity. If this system is not available at the dating service you choose, create a nickname to use on dating sites. It is never a good idea to use your real name. Also consider the implications of the online nickname you use. If you should choose to call yourself by some sort of sexually suggestive nickname (and people do this), you are already inviting a certain type of attention.

Ask for a Photo

Appearance can help you determine whether the person is someone with whom you want to correspond. Most dating sites enable you to post a picture if you like. If the person doesn't send a photo and makes excuses, stop corresponding with them. Don't assume that the person who chats to you on the computer screen will be the same person in real life. The executive you chat with who says he has a body fat rating of 18% and works out every day could very well be a proofreader at a small town newspaper with a wife and several children. Oh, and if you do get a photo, remember that it might not really be current or accurate.

Take Time to Get to Know a Person

Just like when you meet someone new face-to-face, it's always a good idea to get to know the person who you think you might want to eventually meet personally. I know this sounds basic, but if the person you are corresponding with wishes to perpetuate a fantasy, it becomes harder to maintain over time. If you keep asking questions and insisting on answers and proof of those answers, you either drive that person away (that could be a good thing!) or you start to see the real person, which hopefully would also be a very good thing.

Speak on the Phone

Although older rules of etiquette advise women not to push the relationship by calling a man, a phone call can reveal much about a person's social skills. If you decide to speak with someone on the phone, give him your cell phone number or ask the person for his number. Also use telephone-blocking techniques so he can't get your number through caller ID.

Meet in a Public Place

What if you think you have met "the one?" You have chatted online and on the phone for great lengths of time and you both feel it might be

Sandy's tip
If a person displays anger, tries to pressure you, gives inconsistent information about herself (even age!), or refuses to speak to you on the phone after you've established an email correspondence, something isn't right. Check in with your gut reaction. Is it saying something isn't right? If so, trust it. If something feels wrong, it probably is; so move on.

going somewhere; what now? If you met in a traditional sense at work or a social gathering, for example, you already know how to proceed. In this cyber forum you have only been meeting with your minds and the next step must be meeting in person! If you decide to meet, choose a safe place, such as a restaurant during a busy time. Be sure to tell a friend where you're going and what time you plan to return. Give your friend the person's name and phone number. Never arrange for someone to pick you up at your home or office. Take your own transportation. When the date is over, do not allow the person to follow you.

With all of that said, there are many genuine, warm, honest people out there looking for friends and romantic partners. If you follow these guidelines, you should be able to find a multitude to choose from. Have fun!

Online Safety for Children

It happened right here in our quiet, somewhat sedate little village of Pinehurst, North Carolina. A fourteen-year-old girl met a man on the Internet, developed an online relationship, and was lured into running away from home with him. Luckily, this particular story had a happy ending. Even though the girl had erased all the information off her computer, the State Bureau of Investigation (SBI) was still able to use her computer to trace her online footsteps. She was found safe in Louisiana and returned to her family within a few days.

The whole episode sends a shudder down my spine. It makes me realize how vulnerable our children are, how deceptive some grown-ups can be, and how the technology that benefits us in so many ways can be used for evil purposes.

A recent Commerce Department report showed that 90% of the 47.4 million American children aged five to seventeen use the Internet. It doesn't matter anymore whether you live in the big city or a small sleepy town. The Internet is affecting us all.

Software-Assisted Babysitting

How can we keep our children safe? The first thing that most people think of is using a software program to keep children from the shadier side of the Internet. There are some good software programs, such as CyberSitter (found at www.solidoak.com), shown in Figure 9.12, that limit a child's activities on the Internet. You might not, however, have to run out and purchase a software program. Parental controls are built into some of the programs you already use. For instance, Internet Explorer has a Content Advisor that allows you to control the types of content that your computer can gain access to on the Internet. Turn on the Content Advisor by clicking on the Tools menu in Internet Explorer and then clicking on Internet Options. On the Content tab, click on Enable. From there you can set limits for thing such as language, nudity, sex, and violence. You can also set a password so the youngsters cannot change the settings without your permission.

The Safari web browser used on a Mac also has parental controls that help you keep the kids safe online by specifying exactly which websites they can access. You simply choose which websites your children can access by bookmarking only those sites on the Safari Bookmarks Bar. When the parental controls are enabled, the kids can only visit the specified sites. Trying to access any other page gives them an error.

Besides the parental controls that are built into web browsers, your ISP often has free software that can be used to protect the children and grandchildren. AOL is known for its excellent parental controls. Other ISPs, such as Earthlink, also have free software you can use.

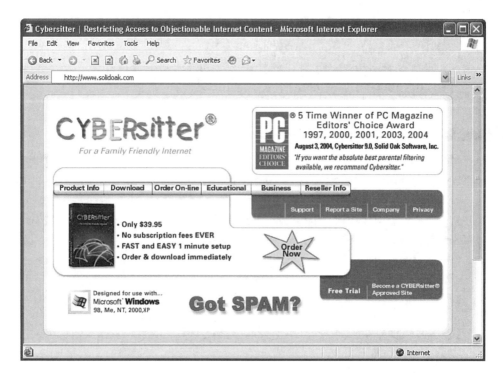

FIGURE 9.12
The Cybersitter software is just one of many software programs that can help keep children safer when they surf the Web.

Offline Steps to Protect the Kids

Using software programs might not be the only step that parental care-takers want to take. The best program for the online safety of children might not be a computer-related program at all. It might well be an old-fashioned program of parental involvement. Based on more than 30 years of computer and parental experience, I propose five simple things that any parent or grandparent can do to help keep their children safe online:

1. Educate your children or grandchildren about Internet safety. Make sure they know it is unwise to give personal information to anyone. Let them know that they should avoid the dark areas of the Web and educate them about the dangers of chat rooms.

Make them aware of the dangers of becoming personally involved with strangers through email, instant messaging, or chatting.

2. If your children or grandchildren use the computer in your home on a regular basis, keep the online computer in a central room in the house, where everyone has full view of the computer screen when it is in use. Be around as much as possible when your children are on the computer. Expect some opposition to this location of the computer. When my own children were growing up, they were not allowed to have either a telephone or television in their bedrooms. I was constantly advised that "everyone else" had these items in their rooms. By forcing the children to use the telephone and television in the main part of the house, I knew what they were watching, who they were talking to, and how much time they invested in each of these activities. How much more important this is with an online computer! A child with an Internet-accessible computer in her bedroom has 24-hour-a-day, unrestricted access to a wealth of pornography and hate sites, not to mention the proximity to many warped grown-ups that go online with the express idea of taking advantage of naïve youngsters.

3. Know the children's passwords. If a child has nothing to hide, he should gladly share his passwords with you. Keep a list of his passwords and occasionally check to make sure that the passwords haven't been changed. Privacy issues come into play here and I don't mean to infer that you should be reading your children's email, but if they know that you can, it might help keep them on the straight and narrow.

4. This important fourth point is not to be overlooked and might, in fact, be the most difficult for some grown-ups. Parents and grandparents should *learn to use the computer*. Investigate, learn, and practice until you know how the computer works and how to use it effectively. As you learn to use the computer, you will find that the computer itself has functions such as history lists that can be used to see which websites a young surfer has recently visited. You will also become more aware of the dangers of the Internet so you can

Sandy's tip
Teenagers are particularly at risk for inappropriate and sometimes dangerous online relationships. If a teen is in your family, check out *Teen Safety on the Information Highway* at www. missingkids.com or order a free copy by calling 1-800-843-5678.

protect your children against them. Remember, a computer-savvy youngster can easily pull the wool over the eyes of an inexperienced computer user. Be sure that you are as proficient on the computer as your children.

5. Investigate what your schools and libraries are doing to make the Internet safe for your children. To find out what you local schools are doing, contact whoever handles Public Information and Community Services for your local school system. Many schools have filtering systems in place. Teachers often have the responsibility of monitoring students whenever they access the Internet on a school computer. Some schools offer a curriculum that will educate children about the lure of the Internet. If you find that your school district is lacking in this area, speak up and make sure your voice is heard.

The Internet was not created as a place to meet people, but it has certainly evolved into just that. Whether you are looking for friendship, support, or a mate, there are places to go and people to meet. So get out there and do it!

Sandy's Summary

We are truly colonizing cyberspace. As we form Internet communities, we are humanizing the Internet and making it our own. Internet communities are websites that are like the corner restaurant, local book clubs, and church groups in our real neighborhoods. In these communities, people with similar interests gather to meet, share stories, and support each other. There are message boards, chat rooms, and Internet groups for all to join and most are free.

If you want even more friendship or are looking for a soul mate, the Internet is available with web services that provide ways to meet people to get as seriously involved as you like. Remember that you must take care when entering any cyber relationship, whether visiting chat room and message boards or frequenting online dating sites. We must look out for the safely of our children and grandchildren as well.

Meeting people on the Internet can fill the gaps in a lonely life, offer personal support when needed, and add spice and companionship to any life. You decide how little or how much you want to get involved, but be sure to get out there and make some new acquaintances.

Sandy Berger

Index

H

O

X - Y - Z